Hooked on Jewelry

Hooked
on Jewelry

40+ Designs to Crochet

Pat Harste

sixth&spring
books

sixth&spring books
233 Spring St.   New York, NY 10013

Book Division Manager **WENDY WILLIAMS**	Yarn Editor **TANIS GRAY**	Vice President, Publisher **TRISHA MALCOLM**
Senior Editor **MICHELLE BREDESON**	Illustrations **PHOEBE ADAMS GAUGHAN**	Production Manager **DAVID JOINNIDES**
Art Director **DIANE LAMPHRON**	Still-Life Photography **DAVID LAZARUS**	Creative Director **JOE VIOR**
Associate Art Director **SHEENA T. PAUL**	Model Photography **ROSE CALLAHAN**	President **ART JOINNIDES**
Instructions Editor **EMILY HARSTE**	Fashion Stylist **JULIE HINES**	
Copy Editor **KRISTINA SIGLER**	Hair and Makeup **INGEBORG K.**	

Library of Congress Control Number: 2008936331

ISBN-13: 978-1-933027-77-7

ISBN-10: 1-933027-77-0

Manufactured in China

1 3 5 7 9 10 8 6 4 2

First Edition

www.sixthandspringbooks.com

To Josephine Keller and Emily Keller Harste. And to all those loving and patient grandmas and moms who taught their kids how to crochet.

Contents

the projects

bonus beadwork earrings

I love to crochet, and I love jewelry even more.

One morning as I was perusing the Sunday papers, I noticed a photo of a silver wire-mesh necklace that looked like it was crocheted, but it wasn't. I whipped out my trusty crochet hook and a ball of silver metallic yarn and tried to duplicate the look. My little experiment not only worked out beautifully, it was super-easy to do and it became the Timeless Tassels necklace in this book. Well, one thing led to another, and before I knew it, I was churning out enough necklaces, bracelets and earrings to fill a small jewelry store.

It's amazing how many ideas for jewelry designs can be found everywhere you look. Books, magazines, TV shows, etc., were all sources of inspiration. It's just a matter of recognizing what's possible with crochet and what's not, and realizing how jewelry findings can make it all come together.

The jewelry ensembles in *Hooked on Jewelry* consist of a necklace accompanied by either earrings and/or a bracelet or two. Despite the intricate appearance of the jewelry, the projects range from easy to intermediate, and most pieces can be made in an evening. Occasionally, I've also included bonus earrings that are not crocheted. They are simply easy-to-assemble coordinating baubles that use leftover beads from the ensemble.

I hope you will be inspired to make many of the projects in this book, and that you will acquire plenty of ideas and techniques to create your own designs. I'm sure you'll get hooked on making crochet jewelry, just as I did!

—Pat Harste

materials and techniques

Crochet Supplies and Tools

Whether you're a beginning crocheter or a seasoned pro, it's a good idea to familiarize, or refamiliarize, yourself with the basic supplies and tools before beginning any of the projects in this book.

Threads

For most of the projects that were made with thread, I used traditional cotton crochet thread or pearl cotton. The rest were made with heavy-weight silk beading thread.

Cotton

In this book I used both crochet cotton and pearl cotton. *Crochet cotton* comes in a variety of thicknesses from size 3 to size 30. A simple guide to follow is: The smaller the number, the thicker the thread, and the larger the number, the thinner the thread. (There are also sizes 40 to 100, but they are generally used for tatting because they are so fine.) With few exceptions, the cotton crochet thread I used for the projects in this book was size 10. Size 10 crochet cotton comes in a good array of colors, including variegated shades. If the color of a project that you have chosen to make is not your thing, you can change it to suit your fancy. Use any manufacturer's size 10 crochet thread to increase your color choices.

Pearl (or perle) cotton is used primarily for embroidery and needlepoint, but it certainly lends itself to small crochet projects such as jewelry. Pearl cotton comes in skeins, in a variety of colors, or in balls, but in limited colors. Though not all companies make all sizes, pearl cotton is available in sizes 3, 5, 8, 12, 16 and 20. Just like crochet cotton, the smaller the number, the thicker the thread, and the higher the number, the thinner the thread. Most cotton projects in this book use size 5.

Easy Weaving
(page 62)
**DMC Size 5
Pearl Cotton**

thread and yarn amounts

● Each project in an ensemble has its own materials list that states the thread or yarn requirements just in case you want to make only that piece. However, you can make all the ensemble projects from the amount listed for the necklace, as long as the rest of the ensemble is made using the same thread or yarn and is in the same color or colors.

Asian Inspiration
(page 42)
**Gudebrod
Champion Silk Thread**

Soft as Suede
(page 38)
**Berroco
Suede yarn**

Victorian Elegance
(page 69)
**Cebelia Size 10
Crochet Cotton**

Silk

I chose Gudebrod Champion Silk Beading Thread for some of the dressier projects. It has a wonderful hand, comes in lovely colors and is available in 14-yard/13-meter cards and 101-yard/92-meter spools. I used size FFF because it's the thickest thread from this manufacturer. However, it's a tad thinner than size 10 crochet cotton, so I don't recommend substituting one for the other.

Yarns

Suede-look, glitzy metallic, silky rayon/cotton and velvety chenille yarns are all featured in this book. I chose these yarns specifically for the look of suede, metal, silk and velvet. If you want to substitute other yarns, you must choose those that are the same weight in order to get similar results, even if the directions state, "Gauge is not important."

Colorful Cloisonné
(page 114)
**Berroco Cotton
Twist yarn**

Timeless Tassels
(page 90)
**Berroco Metallic
FX yarn**

standard yarn weight system

Categories of yarn, gauge ranges, and recommended needle and hook sizes

Yarn Weight Symbol & Category Names	0 Lace	1 Super Fine	2 Fine	3 Light	4 Medium	5 Bulky	6 Super Bulky
Type of Yarns in Category	Fingering 10 count crochet thread	Sock, Fingering, Baby	Sport, Baby	DK, Light Worsted	Worsted, Afghan, Aran	Chunky, Craft, Rug	Bulky, Roving
Knit Gauge Range* in Stockinette Stitch to 4 inches	33–40** sts	27–32 sts	23–26 sts	21–24 sts	16–20 sts	12–15 sts	6–11 sts
Recommended Needle in Metric Size Range	1.5–2.25 mm	2.25–3.25 mm	3.25–3.75 mm	3.75–4.5 mm	4.5–5.5 mm	5.5–8 mm	8 mm and larger
Recommended Needle U.S. Size Range	000 to 1	1 to 3	3 to 5	5 to 7	7 to 9	9 to 11	11 and larger
Crochet Gauge* Ranges in Single Crochet to 4 inch	32–42 double crochets**	21–32 sts	16–20 sts	12–17 sts	11–14 sts	8–11 sts	5–9 sts
Recommended Hook in Metric Size Range	Steel*** 1.6–1.4mm Regular hook 2.25 mm	2.25–3.5 mm	3.5–4.5 mm	4.5–5.5 mm	5.5–6.5 mm	6.5–9 mm	9 mm and larger
Recommended Hook U.S. Size Range	Steel*** 6, 7, 8 Regular hook B–1	B/1 to E/4	E/4 to 7	7 to I/9	I/9 to K/10½	K/10½ to M/13	M/13 and larger

*Guidelines only: The above reflects the most commonly used needle or hook sizes for specific yarn categories.

tip

To use a different yarn from the one specified in a project, look for the yarn symbol in the materials list and substitute a yarn that has the same number to achieve the best results.

15

Crochet Hooks

Crochet hooks come in two classifications: steel (or thread) hooks and yarn hooks.

steel crochet hooks

Steel crochet hooks are typically used with crochet thread. They are always listed from the largest, size 00 (3.5mm), which is used with thicker threads, to the smallest, size 14 (.75mm), which is used with finer threads.

U.S.	METRIC
00	3.5mm
0	3.25mm
1	2.75mm
2	2.25mm
3	2.1mm
4	2mm
5	1.9mm
6	1.8mm
7	1.65mm
8	1.5mm
9	1.4mm
10	1.3mm
11	1.1mm
12	1mm
13	.85mm
14	.75mm

yarn crochet hooks

Yarn crochet hook sizes are always listed from the smallest (used with thinner yarns) to the largest (used with thicker yarns). In the U.S., hooks are sized using letters of the alphabet (except for size 7). The number after the slash is the equivalent knitting needle size.

U.S.	METRIC
B/1	2.25mm
C/2	2.75mm
D/3	3.25mm
E/4	3.5mm
F/5	3.75mm
G/6	4mm
7	4.5mm
H/8	5mm
I/9	5.5mm
J/10	6mm
K/10½	6.5mm
L/11	8mm
M/13	9mm
N/15	10mm
P/16	12mm

Tape measure
for measuring length
and width.

Small, sharp scissors
for cutting thread and yarn.

Straight pins
used to hold pieces together
during assembly.

basic crochet tool kit

Take the time to gather the
tools necessary for making
all of the projects in this
book—it will save you time
in the end. Any tool not
mentioned here that is
required to complete a
project will be listed in the
project's materials list.

Ruler
for measuring
gauge.

Needles
I used a size 26 tapestry needle
(a blunt-tipped needle) for weaving in ends
in most projects. Some projects also
require a size 26 chenille needle
(a sharp-tipped needle) for weaving in ends;
it will be specified in the materials list.
I used a very fine sharps needle
for stringing beads.

**Crochet
hooks**

17

Crochet Techniques

Here are the most basic crochet techniques and stitches you will need to know to make the projects in this book. If you are not already experienced with crochet, it will take some practice to get used to working with a steel crochet hook and fine crochet cotton. You may want to start with a project that uses yarn and a yarn crochet hook, such as the Timeless Tassels necklace on page 90.

Making a Slip Knot

1. Form a loop with your yarn or thread, making sure that the tail of the yarn dangles behind your loop.

2. Insert the crochet hook into the loop and move it under the tail and back out of the loop.

3. Pull on the tail of the yarn to tighten the slip knot on the crochet hook.

Making a Foundation Chain

Do not count loop on hook

1st
2nd
3rd
4th
5th

Do not count slip knot

1. Start by making a slip knot, positioning it near the end of the hook. Wrap the working yarn (the yarn attached to the ball or skein) around the hook as shown. Wrapping the yarn in this way is called a **yarn over** (yo).

2. Draw the yarn through the loop on the hook by catching it with the hook and pulling it toward you.

3. One chain stitch is complete. Lightly tug on the yarn to tighten the loop if it is very loose, or wiggle the hook to loosen the loop if it is tight. Repeat from step 1 to make as many chains as required for your pattern.

4. To count the number of chain stitches made, hold the chain so that the Vs are all lined up. Do not count the loop on the hook or the slip knot you made when beginning the chain. Each V counts as one chain made.

Single Crochet (sc) [UK: double crochet (dc)]

1. Insert the hook under both the front and back loops (i.e., under the complete V) of the 2nd chain from the hook. Wrap the yarn over the hook from back to front (this is called a yarn over) and catch it with the hook. Draw the yarn through the V.

2. You now have two loops on the hook. Yarn over and draw the yarn through both loops on the hook.

3. One single crochet stitch is complete. Continue to repeat steps 1 and 2, inserting the hook into each V across the row.

4. When you reach the end of the row, make one chain stitch (this is called a turning chain), then turn the piece from right to left. To begin the next row, insert the hook under the V of the first stitch (skipping the one chain stitch you just made) and repeat the steps.

Half Double Crochet (hdc) [UK: half treble (htr)]

1. For this stitch, yarn over the hook, then insert it under the V of the 3rd chain stitch from the hook. Yarn over again and draw the yarn through the V.

2. You now have three loops on the hook. Yarn over and draw the hook through all three loops on the hook at once.

3. One half double crochet stitch is complete. Repeat steps 1 and 2 until you reach the end of the row. To proceed to the next row, make two chain stitches and turn.

Illustrations courtesy of *Crochet Today* magazine (www.crochettoday.com)

Double Crochet (dc) [UK: treble (tr)]

1. Yarn over the hook, then insert the hook under the V of the 4th chain stitch from the hook. Yarn over again and catch the yarn, drawing it through the V.

2. You now have three loops on the hook. Yarn over and draw the yarn through the first two loops.

3. You now have two loops remaining on the hook. Yarn over and draw the hook through the two loops.

4. One double crochet stitch is complete. Continue to repeat steps 1 through 3 until you reach the end of the row. To begin the next row, make three chain stitches and turn.

Treble Crochet (tr) [UK: double treble (dtr)]

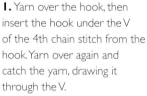

1. Yarn over the hook two times, then insert it under the V of the 5th chain stitch from the hook. Yarn over again and catch the yarn with the hook, drawing it through the V.

2. You now have four loops on the hook. Yarn over and draw through the first two loops (three loops remain on the hook). Yarn over again and draw through the next two loops (two loops remain). Yarn over again and draw through both loops.

3. One treble crochet is complete. Continue to repeat steps 1 and 2 until you reach the end of the row. To begin the next row, make four chain stitches and turn.

Illustrations courtesy of *Crochet Today* magazine (www.crochettoday.com)

Slip Stitch (sl st) [UK: single crochet (sc)]

Insert the hook under the 2nd V from the hook. Yarn over and draw through the V and through the loop on the hook in one movement. One slip stitch is complete.

Fastening Off

1. Cut the yarn or thread, leaving about 4 to 6 inches. Bring the tail from the back to the front over the hook and draw the loose end through the last loop on the hook.

2. Remove the hook and pull the yarn end to tighten and secure it.

terms and abbreviations

approx approximately

beg begin, beginning

CC contrasting color

ch chain(s)

cont continue, continuing

dc double crochet (UK: tr—treble)

dec decrease, decreasing

dtr double treble (UK: trtr—triple treble)

hdc half double crochet (UK: htr—half treble)

inc increase, increasing

lp(s) loop(s)

MC main color

mm millimeter(s)

oz/g ounce(s)/gram(s)

pat(s) pattern(s)

rem remain, remains or remaining

rep repeat, repeating

rev sc reverse single crochet (UK: rev dc—reverse double crochet)

rnd(s) round(s)

RS right side

sc single crochet (UK: dc—double crochet)

sk skip, skipping

sl st slip st (UK: sc—single crochet)

st(s) stitch(es)

t-ch turning chain

tog together

tr treble crochet (UK: dtr—double treble)

tr tr triple treble (UK: qtr—quadruple treble)

WS wrong side

yd/m yard(s)/meter(s)

yo yarn over

* Repeat directions following * as many times as indicated.

[ ] Repeat the directions inside brackets as many times as indicated.

( ) Work directions inside parentheses into stitch indicated.

Jewelry-Making Supplies and Tools

You're sure to feel like a kid in a candy store when you see all the beautiful beads and findings available to choose from. Take some time to familiarize yourself with all the basic materials and tools used in the projects.

Findings

The term "findings" includes everything from jump rings to earwires, and from clasps to bead caps. The findings used in this book are all silver-plated or gold-plated base metals, making them readily available and inexpensive. If you already have some components on hand, such as jump rings and bead caps, and are unsure what size they are, you can measure them against the bead size chart on page 27 to determine their sizes.

Jump rings ⓐ

A jump ring is a circle or oval of wire with an opening. It is used to connect one finding to another or as the loop on which to hook a clasp.

Split rings ⓑ

A split ring is a wire coil with an overlapping opening. Like a jump ring, it is used to connect one finding with another. Key-ring-size split rings figure prominently in the Chain Links three-piece ensemble on page 78.

Eyepins ⓒ

An eyepin is a straight length of wire with an eye (or loop) at one end. For these projects, eyepins are used two ways:

1. To assemble beads to create drop earrings.
2. To secure a cord cap or cone to the end of a crocheted tube

(see Passion for Pearls on page 96 for an example). I called for 1½"/4cm eyepins for all projects that require them. I found this particular length worked perfectly overall.

Headpins ⓓ

A headpin, like an eyepin, is a straight length of wire, but rather than an eye, it has a flattened end that is wider than the thickness of the wire. When you thread on a bead, the flattened end prevents the bead from falling off. Headpins are used primarily to assemble beads to create drop earrings. The end opposite the head is formed into a loop, and the loop is connected to a finding. You will be using 1½"/4cm headpins for all projects that require them.

Cord caps and cones ⓔ

These tube-like metal findings are used to add a finishing touch to the ends of crocheted tubes and slip-stitch crocheted strands. The end of a cord cap or cone has a small hole through which you thread an eyepin or headpin. The end of the pin is then formed into a loop that secures the cord cap or cone in place.

Bead caps ⓕ

A bead cap is a shallow cord cap that is typically used to decorate a bead. For some projects, I used bead caps in place of cord caps.

Clasps

A clasp is simply a finding that fastens a bracelet or necklace. There are four types used in this book, and they range from utilitarian to ornate. Each was chosen for a specific reason.

Springring clasps g

These are the most basic of all clasps. I used them for simple necklaces on which anything fancier would look out of place. I didn't use them for bracelets because they are a little clumsy to operate with one hand.

Lobster-claw clasps h

These clasps are used much like springring clasps, and are great for necklaces but not for bracelets because of the awkwardness of operation. However, they come in a variety of styles and give a more upscale look to a project.

Bar-and-ring toggle clasps i

These clasps are perfect for both necklaces and bracelets, because they are easy to close and open. They come in so many beautiful styles that I considered the choice of clasp part of the overall design of a piece.

Three-hole and five-hole end bars and chain j

These clasps work perfectly for crocheted necklaces because you can neatly sew the ends of the piece to the end bars. The end bars add a decorative touch, and the chain and lobster-claw clasp allows you to adjust the necklace to fit any size neck.

Earwires k and posts l

Earwires are simple wire findings that thread through the ear and are held in place by gravity or hook onto themselves. Earring posts, or earstuds, come in a wide variety of styles from Art Deco to Victorian to ultra modern. The earwires and posts featured in this book all have at least one drop (or loop) from which to hang an assembled bead or other crocheted element.

Earnuts

Earnuts are used to hold post-style earrings in place. Some earrings are sold without earnuts, in which case you must purchase them separately. You can also use earnuts from earrings you already have, if you like.

Ribbon end crimps m

These little clamp-like findings were designed to finish the ends of ribbon, but they work equally well with crochet. They have serrated edges that, when squeezed closed, will attach securely. They also have loops so you can connect the end crimps to another finding.

Crimp beads n

A crimp bead is a small, soft metal bead, which, when flattened or crimped, is used to secure a loop of thread to a jump ring or clasp. It can be flattened using chain-nose pliers or, for a professional finish, crimped using crimping pliers (see "Jewelry-Making Techniques" on page 28).

Chain o

Chain comes in many styles, thicknesses and finishes. Mostly, I chose curb-link and cable-link chains because they are always fashionable and readily available, and because jump rings fit easily through the links for attaching findings. The length required in the materials list is slightly longer than you actually need, because some links will be wasted when you cut the chain into segments. If you plan on recycling an old chain for a project, measure to make sure it is long enough and that links are large enough to accept the size jump ring called for.

tip
Look for plastic multi-compartment boxes in craft stores. Use them to sort and store findings and beads. If possible, store the original packaging with each item so you know exactly what size it is.

CHAIN LINKS
(page 78)

LOVELY
IN LAVENDER
(page 82)

TUMBLING
LEAVES
(page 59)

ART NOUVEAU
RICHE
(page 34)

Beads

There are so many wonderful beads featured in these projects, from acrylic chips to Czech fire-polished faceted beads to faux pearls to real hematite. You can substitute as you like, as long as you use a bead that's the same shape and size. If you already have beads and are unsure of their sizes, simply compare them to the bead size chart opposite to determine their sizes.

wooden beads

● The oval wooden beads I used in this book to cover with crochet are Darice Jewelry Designer Oval Wood Beads X3 in earth tones. Each package contains three sizes: small, medium and large. I used only the medium (18mm x 10mm) and large (20mm x 14mm) sizes (the small size is too tiny). I also used 16mm and 20mm round unfinished wooden beads. All of these beads are available in craft stores or can be ordered online (see "Resources" on page 118).

bead size chart

All sizes are in millimeters

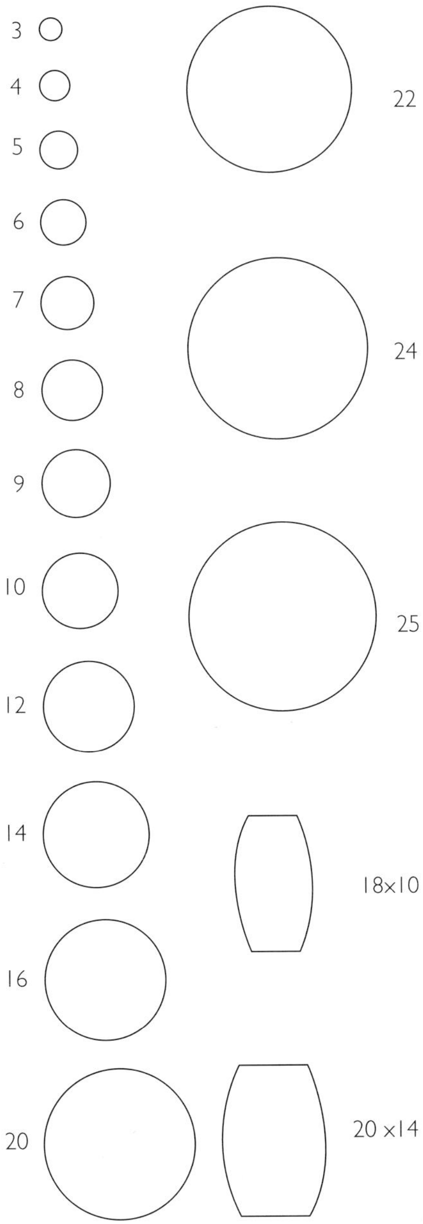

3 ○
4 ○
5 ○
6 ○
7 ○
8 ○
9 ○
10 ○
12 ○
14 ○
16 ○
20 ○

22

24

25

18×10

20×14

Tools

Some designs require tools that are essential to the project's successful completion. Each tool listed below performs one or more special tasks. While these tools can be very expensive, the most inexpensive ones should serve you well.

Wire cutters

Wire cutters are used to cut wire and to trim eyepins and headpins. Do not use them to cut memory wire, as the hard steel will probably nick the cutting edge, thus ruining them forever.

Chain-nose pliers

These pliers are used to shape and bend wire, flatten crimp beads, and open and close jump rings. The inner and outer surfaces are smooth so they will not scratch metal findings. You will need two chain-nose pliers for opening and closing jump rings.

Round-nose pliers

These pliers are used to shape and bend wire into a loop. The inner and outer surfaces are smooth and will not scratch the wire.

Crimping pliers

This specialty tool is used only to crimp a crimp bead. The jaws of the pliers have two notches (a U shape and an O shape) that complete the crimping process neatly and professionally.

Jewelry-Making Techniques

Here are a few basic techniques you'll need to know to complete the projects in this book. It's a good idea to practice how to handle findings and tie knots before assembling your project to get the best-looking and most secure results.

Stringing Beads:
Needle and Thread Technique

Cut a 10"/25.5cm length of sewing thread and thread it onto a size 7 or 8 sharps sewing needle. With thread ends even, make an overhand knot close to the ends (see "Tying Knots" on page 30). This forms the thread into a loop. Working directly from the crochet thread ball, insert the end of the crochet thread through the sewing thread loop for approximately 10"/25.5cm. To transfer each bead onto the crochet thread, simply insert the needle through a bead, then slide the bead down the sewing thread and onto the crochet thread. When all beads have been transferred, remove the sewing needle and thread.

Working With Findings

JUMP RINGS: Opening and closing

You will need two chain-nose pliers. To open a jump ring, hold each side of the jump ring opening in the tips of the pliers. Rotate, moving one pliers toward you and the other pliers away from you. Open the space just wide enough to connect the jump ring to the finding you are working with.

To close the jump ring, repeat the opening instructions but rotate in the opposite direction, making sure the ring is closed completely and there is no gap.

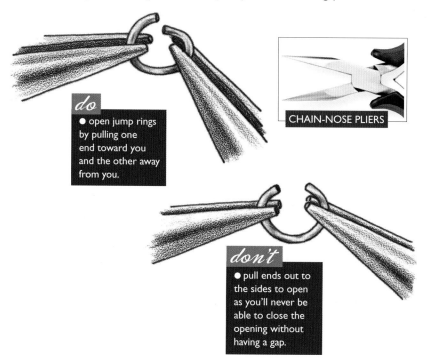

do
● open jump rings by pulling one end toward you and the other away from you.

CHAIN-NOSE PLIERS

don't
● pull ends out to the sides to open as you'll never be able to close the opening without having a gap.

28

EYEPINS AND HEADPINS: Forming end into a loop

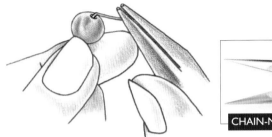

CHAIN-NOSE PLIERS

1. Thread a bead or other component onto an eyepin (or headpin). Holding the bead, pull on the shaft of the eyepin to eliminate any space between the bead and the eye end of the pin. Using wire cutters, trim the end of the eyepin so ⅜"/1 cm extends above the top of the bead. Leaving a tiny bit of space above the bead, use chain-nose pliers to make a slight right angle in the end of the eyepin.

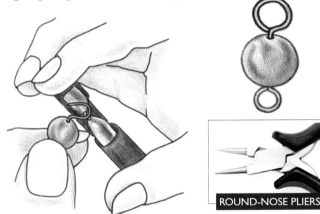

ROUND-NOSE PLIERS

2. Using round-nose pliers, hold the end of the eyepin near the right angle, and bend it into a loop by wrapping it around the top jaw of the pliers. Then continue to bend until the loop is closed.

✸ **Note** If the loop is not centered on the eyepin shaft, adjust its position with chain-nose pliers.

eyepins
SECURING CORD CAPS OR CONES

● An eyepin can be used to secure a cord cap or cone to the end of a crocheted tube (see the Passion for Pearls project on page 96 for an example). Attach the eye to the crocheted fabric following the finishing directions for the project. Thread the cord cap or cone onto the eyepin. Form the opposite end of the eyepin into a loop and connect it to another finding.

split rings
HOW TO OPEN

● All the split rings used in this book are fairly large and easy to open using your thumbnail. If you are worried about breaking your nail or don't want to ruin your manicure, you should consider purchasing a split-ring opener.

To use a split-ring opener, insert the "tooth" of the opener between the overlapping sections of the ring. Connect another split ring, for example, and slide the second split ring around the coils of the first ring. The ring will close back to its original shape once the tool is removed.

CRIMP BEADS: How to crimp

Crimp beads are often used when connecting a string of beads
a clasp. They hold the stringing material securely in place.

CRIMPING PLIERS

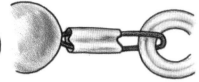

1. Feed the end of the stringing
material through the crimp bead,
through a jump ring and back through
the crimp bead. For basic crimping,
use chain-nose pliers to flatten the
bead and secure it in place. To crimp
using crimping pliers, follow the
next two steps.

2. Squeeze the crimp bead in the
U notch of the crimping pliers to set
it in place.

3. Position the crimp bead in the
O notch and rotate it so the seam
created by the U notch is on its side.
Now squeeze the pliers to further
secure and shape it. Once the crimp
bead is in position, follow the finishing
directions for the individual project.

tying knots

I used a couple of common knots in some of the projects in this book. Here's how to make them.

Basic overhand knot

OVERHAND KNOT

This is one of the most basic knots. To tie a knot with a single
strand of thread, pass the left end of the thread over and under
the right end. Pull on the ends to tighten.

In some of the projects in this book, this knot is used to tie
together two thread ends, often to secure a bead. Hold the
ends together, making sure they are even. Wrap the ends around
your left index and middle fingers to form a loop. Thread the
ends through the loop, forming a loose knot, then drop the loop
from your fingers. Move the knot toward the base of the bead,
then pull on the ends to tighten the knot.

SQUARE KNOT

A square knot is a very secure, all-purpose knot.

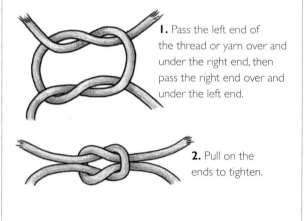

1. Pass the left end of
the thread or yarn over and
under the right end, then
pass the right end over and
under the left end.

2. Pull on the
ends to tighten.

SIMPLY CHARMING
(page 102)

the projects

art nouveau riche

Iridescent peacock-colored seed beads give this ensemble of tubular crochet necklace and earrings the look of Tiffany art glass. The Art Nouveau era's love of natural forms is represented by the dragonfly clasp that fastens the necklace and the sunflowers that adorn the earrings.

Iridescent Bead Necklace

Finished Measurements

- Length approx 32"/81cm (including clasp)
- Width approx ⅜"/1cm

Materials

- 1 ball (approx 284yd/260m) of DMC Inc. *Cebelia Size 10 Crochet Cotton* (mercerized cotton) in #310 black
- Size 2 (2.25mm) steel crochet hook *or size to obtain gauge*
- Two 40g boxes (or nine hundred sixty-five) of Matsuno Iris Round 6/0 seed beads in peacock
- One 38 x 5mm antique silver cast-pewter dragonfly loop
- One 40 x 27mm antique silver cast-pewter dragonfly hook
- Two 22mm antique silver pewter lacy mesh cones
- Two 3mm round silver-plated beads
- Two 1½"/4cm silver-plated eyepins
- Chain-nose pliers

Stitch Glossary

SLB Slide bead next to crochet hook.

sc2tog [Insert hook in next st, yo and draw up a lp] twice, yo and draw through all 3 lps on hook.

- Round-nose pliers
- Wire cutters
- Any color sewing thread
- Size 7 or 8 sharps sewing needle

Gauge

5 sts to ½"/1.3cm diameter and 26 rnds to 4"/10cm over tubular crochet using size 2 (2.25mm) steel crochet hook.
Take time to check your gauge.

Necklace

Stringing beads

Using needle and thread technique, string all seed beads onto crochet thread.

Tubular crochet

Ch 3. Join ch with a sl st forming a ring.

Rnd 1 Work 5 sc in ring. Do not join. You will be working in a spiral where rnds are not joined.

Rnd 2 [Insert hook in next st, SLB, yo and draw up a lp, yo and draw through both lps on hook] 5 times. You will now be working from the WS.

Rnd 3 [Insert hook under horizontal thread coming out of RH side of next bead of rnd below, SLB, yo and draw up a lp, yo and draw through both lps on hook] 5 times. Rep rnd 3 for tubular crochet and work until all beads are used.

Next rnd [Insert hook under horizontal thread coming out of RH side of next bead of rnd below, yo and draw up a lp, yo and draw through both lps on hook] 5 times.

Last rnd Sc in next st, [sc2tog] twice. Fasten off.

Finishing

Weave in ends.

Assembling necklace

Open loop end of an eyepin. Insert shaft of eyepin through center of one end of crocheted tube. Draw eyepin through, hooking the crocheted fabric with the open loop. Close the loop, securing the eyepin to the fabric. Thread on a cone, then a 3mm bead. Form end of eyepin into a loop and connect it to dragonfly hook. Rep at opposite end connecting eyepin loop to dragonfly loop.

Iridescent Bead Earrings

Finished Measurement
● Length approx 2½"/6.5cm

Materials
● 1 ball (approx 284yd/260m) of DMC Inc. *Cebelia Size 10 Crochet Cotton* (mercerized cotton) in #310 black
● Size 2 (2.25mm) steel crochet hook *or size to obtain gauge*
● Eighty Matsuno Iris Round 6/0 seed beads in peacock
● One pair 18mm diameter antique silver flower cast-pewter earstuds with drops
● Two 22mm antique silver cast-pewter lacy mesh cones
● Two 3mm round silver-plated beads
● Two 1½"/4cm silver-plated eyepins
● Chain-nose pliers
● Round-nose pliers
● Wire cutters

Stitch Glossary

SLB Slide bead next to crochet hook.

sc2tog [Insert hook in next st, yo and draw up a lp] twice, yo and draw through all 3 lps on hook.

● Any color sewing thread
● Size 7 or 8 sharps sewing needle

Gauge
4 sts to ⅜"/1cm diameter and 10 rnds to 1½"/4cm over tubular crochet using size 2 (2.25mm) steel crochet hook.
Take time to check your gauge.

Earrings (make 2)
Stringing beads
Using needle and thread technique, string forty seed beads onto crochet thread.
Tubular crochet
To make an adjustable ring, make a slip knot 10"/25.5cm from free end of crochet thread. Place slip knot on hook, then wrap free end of thread twice around the first and second fingers of your left hand. Now work from thread coming from ball as foll:

Rnd 1 Beg at bottom of earring, work 4 sc in ring, pull free end of yarn to close circle. Do not join. You will be working in a spiral where rnds are not joined.

Rnd 2 [Insert hook in next st, SLB, yo and draw up a lp, yo and draw through both lps on hook] 4 times. You will now be working from the WS.

Rnd 3 [Insert hook under horizontal thread coming out of RH side of next bead of rnd below, SLB, yo and draw up a lp, yo and draw through both lps on hook] 4 times. Rep rnd 3 for tubular crochet and work until all beads are used.

Next rnd [Insert hook under horizontal thread coming out of RH side of next bead of rnd below, yo and draw up a lp, yo and draw through both lps on hook] 4 times.

Last rnd [Sc2tog] twice. Fasten off for top of crocheted tube.

Finishing
Weave in ends.
Assembling earrings
For each earring, open loop end of an eyepin. Insert shaft of eyepin through center top of a crocheted tube. Draw eyepin through, hooking the crocheted fabric with the open loop. Close the loop, securing the eyepin to the fabric. Thread on a cone, then a 3mm bead. Form end of eyepin into a loop and connect it to earstud drop.

There are so many colors of iridescent seed beads to choose from, and each will give this ensemble a different look.

soft as suede

Dark jewel-tone shades of suede-like yarn make this multi-strand necklace, chunky bangles and fabulous double-hoop earrings must-haves for your wardrobe.

Multi-Strand Necklace

Finished Measurements
- Length approx 30"/76cm (including clasp)
- Width at center approx 8½"/21.5cm

Materials
- 1 1¾oz/50g ball (approx 120yd/111m) of Berroco, Inc. *Suede* (nylon 4) in #3769 sundance kid
- Size G/6 (4mm) crochet hook
- Fourteen 1⅛"/28.5mm cabone rings (also called bone rings)
- Thirty-two 6 x 5mm silver-plated smooth-finish ribbon end crimps
- Thirty 6mm round silver-plated jump rings
- Four 8 x 6mm oval silver-plated jump rings
- One 36"/91.5cm length of 5.5mm silver-plated twisted cable chain
- One 20 x 16mm antique silver cast-pewter bar-and-ring toggle clasp
- Two chain-nose pliers
- Wire cutters
- Size 26 chenille needle

Gauge
Gauge is not important.

❋ **Note** You will find it helpful to use pliers to pull the chenille needle through when weaving in ends.

Necklace
Covering cabone rings (make 14)
Make a slip knot, leaving a 6"/15cm tail, and place on hook.

Rnd 1 (RS) Working fairly tightly, sc over cabone ring until ring is completely covered. Do not join. Cut yarn leaving a 6"/15cm end. Do not fasten off, just draw end through last st. Thread end in chenille needle. Insert needle into top of first sc, draw yarn through (this is the seam edge). On WS, weave in end. Weave in rem end.

Finishing
Attaching end crimps
With WS of covered ring facing, insert the seam edge into the crimp. Position the crimp so it is perpendicular to the edge of the ring and the teeth of the crimp are embedded in the crocheted fabric. Squeeze the crimp closed using pliers. Squeeze at right-side edge of crimp, then at left-side edge to ensure an even closure. Attach the second end crimp to the opposite edge. Continue to work in this manner, attaching two end crimps to eleven more covered rings. For the two corner connecting rings, attach three end crimps, spaced ⅛"/.3cm apart, to one edge of a covered ring. On opposite edge, attach one crimp, centered on the opposite three crimps.

Assembling necklace
Cut fifteen 5-link (approx 1½"/4cm) lengths of chain. When connecting each of the three strands, take care that RS of covered rings face out and that chain lies flat and is not twisted. For top strand, connect three covered rings to two lengths of chain using round jump rings, then connect a length of chain to first and last covered rings. For center strand, connect four covered rings to

three lengths of chain, then connect a length of chain to first and last covered rings. For bottom strand, connect five covered rings to four lengths of chain, then connect a length of chain to first and last covered rings. Working from the top strand to the bottom, connect end chains to the three end crimps on the corner connecting rings.

Cut two 21-link (approx 6⅜"/16cm) lengths of chain. Using oval jump rings, connect chains to the single end crimps on the corner connecting rings. Connect each portion of toggle clasp to a chain using an oval jump ring.

Double-Hoop Earrings

Finished Measurement
● Length approx 4⅜"/11cm

Materials
● 1 1¾oz/50g ball (each approx 120yd/111m) each of Berroco, Inc. *Suede* (nylon (**4**)) in #3769 sundance kid (A), #3745 calamity jane (B) and #3715 tonto (C)
● Size G/6 (4mm) crochet hook
● Two 1⅛"/28.5mm cabone rings (also called bone rings)
● Two 1½"/38mm cabone rings
● One pair 12mm half-ball silver-plated earstuds with drops

● Two silver-plated barrel earnuts
● Six 6 x 5mm silver-plated smooth-finish ribbon end crimps
● Four 8 x 6mm oval silver-plated jump rings
● Two chain-nose pliers
● Size 26 chenille needle

Gauge
Gauge is not important.

✱ **Note** You will find it helpful to use pliers to pull the chenille needle through when weaving in ends.

Earrings (make 2)
Covering small cabone rings
With A, make a slip knot, leaving a 6"/15cm tail, and place on hook.

Rnd 1 (RS) Working fairly tightly, sc over smaller cabone ring until ring is completely covered. Do not join. Cut yarn leaving a 6"/15cm end. Do not fasten off, just draw end through last st. Thread end in chenille needle. Insert needle into top of first sc, draw yarn through (this is the seam edge). On WS, weave in end. Weave in rem end.

Covering large cabone rings
With B, make a slip knot leaving a 6"/15cm tail, and place on hook.

Rnd 1 (RS) Working fairly tightly, sc over large cabone ring until ring is completely covered. Cont to work as for small cabone rings.

Finishing
Attaching end crimps
For each small covered ring, work as foll: With WS of covered ring facing, insert the seam edge into the crimp. Position the crimp so it is perpendicular to the edge of the ring and the teeth of the crimp are embedded in the crocheted fabric. Squeeze the crimp closed using pliers. Squeeze at right-side edge of crimp, then at left-side edge to ensure an even closure. Attach the second end crimp on the opposite edge. For each large covered ring, attach end crimp to one seam edge only.

Embroidery
With C, sew a row of running sts, going over and under post of sts around perimeter of each covered ring.

Assembling earrings
For each earring, connect A and B rings with an oval jump ring making sure that RS of covered rings face out. Connect A ring to earstud drop with an oval jump ring.

Chunky Bangle Bracelets

Finished Measurements
- Inner circumference approx 7⅞"/20cm
- Outer circumference approx 11½"/29cm

Materials
- 1 1¾oz/50g ball (each approx 120yd/111m) each of Berroco, Inc. *Suede* (nylon (**4**)) in #3745 calamity jane (A), #3715 tonto (B) and #3769 sundance kid (C)
- Size G/6 (4mm) crochet hook *or size to obtain gauge*
- Polyester fiberfill

Gauge
20 sts and 24 rows to 4"/10cm over sc using size G/6 (4mm) crochet hook.
Take time to check your gauge.

Bracelets (make 3)

With A, ch 8.

Rnd 1 Taking care not to twist the ch, sc in first ch and in each ch around forming a ring. You will be working in a spiral where rnds are not joined and you do not ch to beg each rnd.

Rnd 2 Sc in each st around.

Rep rnd 2 for pat st and work even until piece measures 9½"/24cm from beg. Fasten off. Make 2 more bangles using B and C.

Finishing

To stuff each bangle, first pull out very small tufts from fiberfill package. Working from one end of the bangle, then the other, use the end of the crochet hook to insert fiberfill tufts inside. Stuff fairly firmly, but take care not to stretch out sts or rows. Whipstitch ends of the bangle tog, stuffing any empty spaces before stitching opening closed.

asian inspiration

Evoking the allure of the Far East, a faux-cinnabar medallion is suspended from silky ties that are flecked with real jade beads. Complete the look with a tubular crochet bracelet made with jade, matte seed and cinnabar beads.

Medallion Necklace

Finished Measurements
- Length approx 20"/50cm (excluding ties)
- Width of strap approx ⅝"/1.6cm

Materials
- 1 spool (approx 101yd/93m) of *Gudebrod Champion Silk Thread Size FFF* in black
- Size 2 (2.25mm) steel crochet hook *or size to obtain gauge*
- One 2¼"/57mm round synthetic cinnabar Chinese medallion
- Thirty-four 4mm round African jade beads
- Any color sewing thread
- Size 7 or 8 sharps sewing needle
- Small safety pin

Stitch Glossary
SLB Slide bead next to crochet hook.

sc2tog [Insert hook in next st, yo and draw up a lp] twice, yo and draw through all 3 lps on hook.

sc3tog [Insert hook in next st, yo and draw up a lp] 3 times, yo and draw through all 4 lps on hook.

Gauge
One rep to ¾" x ¾"/2cm x 2cm over one bead pat st using size 2 (2.25mm) steel crochet hook.
Take time to check your gauge.

Necklace
Right strap
Stringing beads
Using needle and thread technique, string 12 beads onto silk thread.

Joining to medallion
Ch 10.

Row 1 Sc in 2nd ch from hook and in each ch across—9 sts. Turn.

Rows 2–11 Ch 1, sc in each st across. Turn. When row 11 is completed, remove lp from hook, then fasten with safety pin. With RS of medallion facing and safety pin at your right, insert bottom edge of piece through upper right slit in medallion. Remove safety pin, then place lp back on hook. Bring bottom edge of piece up to meet top edge.

Next row (RS) Insert hook into first st of top edge and corresponding bottom lp of foundation ch, then sc tog. Cont to work as foll: *sc next st of top edge tog with next bottom lp of foundation ch; rep from * across—9 sts. Turn.

Beg bead pat st
Row 1 (WS) Ch 1, sc2tog, sc in next 5 sts, sc2tog—7 sts. Turn.

Row 2 Ch 1, sc2tog, sc in next 3 sts, sc2tog—5 sts. Turn.

Row 3 Ch 1, sc2tog, sc in next st, sc2tog—3 sts. Turn.

Row 4 Ch 1, sc3tog—1 st. Turn.

Row 5 Ch 1, SLB, sc in st. Turn.

Row 6 Ch 1, work 3 sc in st. Turn.

Row 7 Ch 1, work 2 sc in first st, sc in next st, work 2 sc in last st—5 sts. Turn.

Row 8 Ch 1, work 2 sc in first st, sc in next 3 sts, work 2 sc in last st—7 sts. Turn.

Row 9 Ch 1, work 2 sc in first st, sc in next 5 sts, work 2 sc in last st—9 sts. Turn.

Row 10 Ch 1, sc in each st across. Turn. Rep rows 1–10 10 times more, then rows 1–5 once. When row 5 is completed, do not turn.

Tie

Next row Ch 1, *working from right to left, insert hook under 2 vertical threads of sc below ch-1 just made. Yo and draw through a lp, yo and draw through 2 lps on hook, ch 1; rep from * until tie measures 12"/30.5cm from beg. Fasten off, leaving a long tail.

Left strap

Stringing beads

Using needle and thread technique, string 12 beads onto silk thread.

Joining to medallion

Ch 10.

Row 1 Sc in 2nd ch from hook and in each ch across—9 sts. Turn.

Rows 2–11 Ch 1, sc in each st across. Turn. When row 11 is completed, remove lp from hook, then fasten with safety pin. With RS of medallion facing and safety pin at your right, insert bottom edge of piece through upper left slit in medallion. Cont to work as for right strap.

Tassel

Ch 2, leaving a long tail.

Row 1 Working from right to left, insert hook under 2 vertical threads of 2nd ch from hook, yo and draw through a lp, yo and draw through 2 lps on hook. Do not turn.

Row 2 Ch 1, *working from right to left, insert hook under 2 vertical threads of sc below ch-1 just made. Yo and draw through a lp, yo and draw through 2 lps on hook, ch 1; rep from * until piece measures 8½"/21.5cm from beg. Fasten off leaving a long tail.

Finishing

Weave in beg ends of right and left straps. Working on a thick terry towel, press each strap and tie from the WS using a dampened pressing cloth. Press tassel flat.

Stringing beads

For each strap tie, string 3 beads onto tail using needle and thread technique. Make a firm overhand knot close to last bead to secure beads in place. Cut off excess tail ¼"/.6cm from knot. For each tassel tail, string on 2 beads; make overhand knot close to last bead to secure. Cut off excess tail ¼"/.6cm from knot. Working from RS to WS, thread ends of tassel through bottom of medallion, as shown in photo. With ends of tassel even, make an overhand knot close to bottom of medallion.

bonus earrings

For each earring, thread a 4mm African jade bead, 22mm flat diamond cinnabar bead and another 4mm African jade bead onto a 1½"/4cm silver-plated headpin. Make a loop at end of headpin connecting it to a medium, kidney-shaped silver earwire.

Jade and Cinnabar Bracelet

Finished Measurements
- Inner circumference approx 6¼"/16cm
- Outer circumference approx 8½"/22cm

Materials
- 1 ball (approx 284yd/260m) of DMC Inc. *Cebelia Size 10 Crochet Cotton* (mercerized cotton) in #310 black
- Size 2 (2.25mm) steel crochet hook *or size to obtain gauge*
- Eighty-two 4mm round African jade beads
- Eighty 6/0 black matte seed beads
- One 22mm flat diamond cinnabar bead
- Two 8mm silver-plated cord caps
- Three 1½"/4cm silver-plated eyepins
- Chain-nose pliers
- Round-nose pliers
- Wire cutters

Stitch Glossary
SLB Slide bead next to crochet hook.

sc2tog [Insert hook in next st, yo and draw up a lp] twice, yo and draw through all 3 lps on hook.

- Any color sewing thread
- Size 7 or 8 sharps sewing needle

Gauge
4 sts to ½"/1.3cm diameter and 40 rnds to 6½"/16.5cm over tubular crochet using size 2 (2.25mm) steel crochet hook.

Take time to check your gauge.

Bracelet
Stringing beads
Set aside two jade beads for finishing. Using needle and thread technique, string eighty jade beads and eighty seed beads onto crochet thread as foll: *one jade bead, one seed bead; rep from * until all beads are strung.

Tubular crochet
Ch 3. Join ch with a sl st forming a ring.

Rnd 1 Work 4 sc in ring. Do not join. You will be working in a spiral where rnds are not joined.

Rnd 2 [Insert hook in next st, SLB, yo and draw up a lp, yo and draw through both lps on hook] 4 times. You will now be working from the WS.

Rnd 3 [Insert hook under horizontal thread coming out of RH side of next bead of rnd below, SLB, yo and draw up a lp, yo and draw through both lps on hook] 4 times. Rep rnd 3 for tubular crochet and work until all beads are used.

Next rnd [Insert hook under horizontal thread coming out of RH side of next bead of rnd below, yo and draw up a lp, yo and draw through both lps on hook] 4 times.

Last rnd [Sc2tog] twice. Fasten off.

Finishing
Weave in ends.
Attaching cord caps
Open loop end of an eyepin. Insert shaft of eyepin through center of one end of crocheted tube. Draw eyepin through, hooking the crocheted fabric with the open loop. Close the loop, securing the eyepin to the fabric. Thread on a cord cap. Form end of eyepin into a loop. Rep at opposite end of crocheted tube.
Assembling bracelet
Connect rem eyepin to a crocheted tube loop. On this eyepin, thread a jade bead, cinnabar bead and rem jade bead. Form end of eyepin into a loop, connecting it to rem crocheted tube loop.

out of africa

Strands and strands of earthy ethnic beads make a stunning jewelry statement. Enhance the look with a chunky tubular crochet bracelet and leafy bonus earrings.

Beaded Twist Bracelet

Finished Measurements
- Inner circumference approx 6⅞"/17.5cm
- Outer circumference approx 11"/28cm

Materials
- 1 ball (approx 300yd/275m) of South Maid/Coats & Clark *Size 10 Crochet Cotton* (cotton) in #12 black
- Size 2 (2.25mm) steel crochet hook *or size to obtain gauge*
- One hundred forty 6mm round acrylic beads in brown
- Seventy 8mm flat round antique acrylic beads
- Seventy 4mm round acrylic beads in light brown
- Two 24 x 16mm flat teardrop antique acrylic beads
- Any color sewing thread
- Size 7 or 8 sharps sewing needle

Stitch Glossary

SLB Slide bead next to crochet hook.

sc2tog [Insert hook in next st, yo and draw up a lp] twice, yo and draw through all 3 lps on hook.

Gauge

8 sts to 1"/2.5cm diameter and 35 rnds to 10½"/26.5cm over tubular crochet using size 2 (2.25mm) steel crochet hook.

Take time to check your gauge.

Bracelet

Stringing beads
Using needle and thread technique, string beads onto crochet thread as foll: *one 4mm, one 6mm, one 8mm, one 6mm; rep from * until all beads are strung.

Tubular crochet
Ch 4. Join ch with a sl st forming a ring.

Rnd 1 Work 8 sc in ring. Do not join. You will be working in a spiral where rnds are not joined.

Rnd 2 [Insert hook in next st, SLB, yo and draw up a lp, yo and draw through both lps on hook] 8 times. You will now be working from the WS.

Rnd 3 [Insert hook under horizontal thread coming out of RH side of next bead of rnd below, SLB, yo and draw up a lp, yo and draw through both lps on hook] 8 times. Rep rnd 3 for tubular crochet and work until all beads are used.

Next rnd [Insert hook under horizontal thread coming out of RH side of next bead of rnd below, yo and draw up a lp, yo and draw through both lps on hook] 8 times.

Last rnd [Sc2tog] 4 times. Fasten off.

Finishing
Weave in ends.

Tie
With 3 strands of thread held tog, make a chain 6½"/16.5cm long. Fasten off. Using steel crochet hook, draw each end of tie through each end of bracelet. At each end of tie, thread on a flat teardrop bead. Knot end in an overhand knot to secure bead. Trim ends ⅜"/1cm from knot. Tie the tie once.

LEAF BEAD NECKLACE

BEAD ROPE NECKLACE

BEADED TWIST BRACELET

Leaf Bead Necklace

Finished Measurement

- Length before tying approx 31"/78.5cm (excluding ties)

Materials

- 1 ball (approx 100yd/91m) of J. P. Coats/Coats & Clark *Speed-Cro-Sheen Size 3 Crochet Cotton* (cotton) in #3 black

- Size F/5 (3.75mm) crochet hook
- Twenty 40 x 14mm antique leaf acrylic drop beads
- Two 8mm flat round antique acrylic beads
- Any color sewing thread
- Size 7 or 8 sharps sewing needle

Stitch Glossary

SLB (slide bead) Slide bead next to crochet hook. Make next ch using thread coming from opposite side of bead hole.

Gauge

Gauge is not important.

Necklace

Thread all leaf beads onto crochet thread using the needle and thread technique. Make a slip knot 10"/25.5cm from free end of thread. Place slip knot on hook.

Row 1 Ch 28, *SLB, ch 5; rep from * until all beads are used, end ch 23. Fasten off, leaving a 10"/25.5cm end.

Finishing

To fasten necklace, tie ends in an overhand knot. For each thread end, make an overhand knot 2½"/6.5cm from fastening knot. Using the needle and thread technique, string on an 8mm bead. Make an overhand knot close to bottom of bead. Trim end ½"/1.3cm from knot.

Bead Rope Necklaces

Finished Measurements

Short necklace
- Length approx 25"/63.5cm (excluding ties)

Long necklace
- Length approx 29"/73.5cm (excluding ties)

Materials

- 1 ball (approx 300yd/275m) of South Maid/Coats & Clark. *Size 10 Crochet Cotton* (cotton) in #12 black
- Size 2 (2.25mm) steel crochet hook
- Seventy-nine 8mm flat round antique acrylic beads (thirty-eight for short necklace and forty-one for long necklace)
- Any color sewing thread
- Size 7 or 8 sharps sewing needle

Stitch Glossary

SLB (slide bead) Slide bead next to crochet hook. Make next ch using thread coming from opposite side of bead hole.

Gauge

Gauge is not important.

Short Necklace

Thread thirty-eight beads onto crochet thread using the needle and thread technique. Make a slip knot and place on hook.

Row 1 Ch 38, *SLB, ch 3; rep from * until all beads are used, end ch 35. Fasten off.

Long Necklace

Thread forty-one beads onto crochet thread using the needle and thread technique. Make a slip knot and place on hook.

Row 1 Ch 38, *SLB, ch 4; rep from * until all beads are used, end ch 34. Fasten off.

Finishing

To fasten each necklace, make an overhand knot 1"/2.5cm from the ends.

Oval Bead Necklace

Finished Measurement

• Length before tying approx 27"/68.5cm (excluding ties)

Materials

• 1 ball (approx 100yd/91m) of J. P. Coats/Coats & Clark *Speed-Cro-Sheen* Size 3 Crochet Cotton (cotton) in #3 black
• Size G/6 (4mm) crochet hook
• Seven 27 x 18mm oval antique acrylic beads
• Four 8mm flat round antique acrylic beads
• Any color sewing thread
• Size 7 or 8 sharps sewing needle

Gauge

Gauge is not important.

Necklace

With 2 strands of thread held tog, make a slip knot 10"/25.5cm from free ends. Place slip knot on hook. Make a chain 38"/96.5cm long. Fasten off leaving a 10"/25.5cm end.

Finishing
Assembling necklace

String an oval bead onto chain. Position bead in center, then make an overhand knot each side of bead to secure. Working one side of center bead at a time, *make an overhand knot 1½"/4cm from last knot, string on an oval bead, make an overhand knot close to bead; rep from * twice more. Rep on opposite side.

To fasten necklace, tie free ends in an overhand knot close to ends of chain. On each free end, make an overhand knot 1½"/4cm from fastening knot. Using the needle and thread technique, string on an 8mm bead. Make an overhand knot close to bottom of bead. Trim end ½"/1.3cm from knot.

Clamshell Bead Necklace

Finished Measurement

• Length before tying approx 25"/63.5cm (excluding thread ends)

Materials

• 1 ball (approx 100yd/91m) of J. P. Coats/Coats & Clark *Speed-Cro-Sheen* Size 3 Crochet Cotton (cotton) in #3 black
• Size F/5 (3.75mm) crochet hook
• Twenty-five 21 x 13mm antique clamshell acrylic drop beads
• Any color sewing thread
• Size 7 or 8 sharps sewing needle

Stitch Glossary

SLB (slide bead) Slide bead next to crochet hook. Make next ch using thread coming from opposite side of bead hole.

Gauge

Gauge is not important.

Necklace

Thread all beads onto crochet thread using the needle and thread technique. Make a slip knot 8"/20.5cm from free end of thread. Place slip knot on hook.

Row 1 Ch 16, *SLB, ch 4; rep from * until all beads are used, end ch 12. Fasten off leaving an 8"/20.5cm end.

Finishing

To fasten necklace, tie ends in a firm square knot. Weave in ends.

bonus earrings (make 2)

For each earring, use a 7mm gold-plated jump ring to connect a 40 x 14mm antique leaf acrylic drop bead to a 1½"/4cm gold-plated eyepin. Onto same eyepin, thread a 4mm light brown acrylic bead, an 8mm flat round antique acrylic bead and another 4mm light brown acrylic bead. Make a loop at end of eyepin and connect it to a gold-filled French hoop earwire.

CLAMSHELL BEAD NECKLACE

OVAL BEAD BRACELET

Wear each necklace separately or all five together for a bold and beautiful look.

jet set

The extra-long, lariat-style necklace of sparkling jet beads is an elegant and versatile accessory. Make it a set by adding long, twisted earrings.

Beaded Lariat Necklace

Finished Measurements
- Length (before tying) approx 49"/124.5cm (including tassels)
- Width approx ⅜"/1cm

Materials
- 1 spool (approx 101yd/93m) of Gudebrod *Champion Silk Thread Size FFF* in black
- Size 2 (2.25mm) steel crochet hook *or size to obtain gauge*
- Four 16"/40.5cm strands (approx one hundred four beads per strand) of 4mm round Czech fire-polished faceted beads in jet
- Four 18 x 9mm terbium glass teardrops in jet
- Two 22 x 11mm terbium glass teardrops in jet
- Any color sewing thread
- Size 7 or 8 sharps sewing needle
- Small safety pin

Stitch Glossary
SLB Slide bead next to crochet hook.

SLST Slide small teardrop bead next to crochet hook.

SLLT Slide large teardrop next to crochet hook.

Gauge
1 st to ⅜"/1cm and 40 rows to 4"/10cm over bead pat st using size 2 (2.25mm) steel crochet hook.

Take time to check your gauge.

Necklace
Stringing beads
Using needle and thread technique, string four hundred sixteen 4mm beads onto silk thread.

Beg bead pat st
Make a slip knot, leaving a 1½yd/1.5m tail for second beaded tassel. Place slip knot on hook.

Row 1 Ch 1, SLB, ch 1. Turn.

Row 2 Sc in 2nd ch from hook, SLB, ch 1. Turn.

Row 3 Sc in st, SLB, ch 1. Turn. Rep row 3 until all beads are used. Do not fasten off. Place lp on hook onto safety pin. Cut silk thread leaving a 1½yd/1.5m tail for first beaded tassel.

First Beaded Tassel
Beg with tail just cut, use needle and thread technique to string a small teardrop bead, large teardrop bead and small teardrop bead onto tail. Place lp on safety pin back onto crochet hook. Turn. Sc in center of st of 2 rows below for starting point of tassel.

First fringe

Ch 15, SLST, ch 1, turn.

Row 1 Working through back lps of ch, sl st in first ch from hook and in each of next 14 ch. Sc in starting point.

Second fringe

Ch 22, SLLT, ch 1, turn.

Row 1 Working through back lps of ch, sl st in first ch from hook and in each of next 21 ch. Sc in starting point.

Third fringe

Work same as for first fringe. Fasten off.

Second Beaded Tassel

Use needle and thread technique to string a small teardrop bead, rem large teardrop bead and rem small teardrop bead onto beg tail. Insert hook into center of st of 2 rows below, yo and draw up a lp, yo and draw through 2 lps on hook. This is starting point of tassel. Beg with first fringe, work same as for first beaded tassel.

Finishing

Weave in ends. Working on a thick terry towel, press necklace and tassels using a damp pressing cloth.

Beaded Dangle Earrings

Finished Measurement

- Length approx 2¾"/7cm

Materials

- 1 card (approx 14yd/13m) of Gudebrod *Champion Silk Thread Size FFF* in black
- Size 2 (2.25mm) steel crochet hook *or size to obtain gauge*
- One pair antique silver post earrings with drops
- Twenty-four 4mm round Czech fire-polished faceted beads in jet
- Two 18 x 9mm terbium glass teardrops in jet
- Two silver-plated 8 x 3mm prong bails
- Four 4mm silver-plated jump rings
- Two chain-nose pliers

Stitch Glossary

SLT Slide teardrop bead next to crochet hook.

SLB Slide bead next to crochet hook.

- Any color sewing thread
- Size 7 or 8 sharps sewing needle

Gauge

1 st to ⅜"/1cm and 10 rows to 1"/2.5cm over bead pat st using size 2 (2.25mm) steel crochet hook.

Take time to check your gauge.

Earrings (make 2)

Stringing beads

Using needle and thread technique, string twelve 4mm beads and one teardrop bead onto silk thread.

Beg bead pat st

Make a slip knot, leaving a long tail. Place slip knot on hook.

Row 1 SLT, ch 2. Turn.

Row 2 Sc in 2nd ch from hook, SLB, ch 1. Turn.

Row 3 Sc in st, SLB, ch 1. Turn. Rep row 3 until all beads are used. Fasten off.

Finishing

Weave in ends. Do not press. Allow crocheted strip to twist.

Assembling earrings

For each earring, position bail over center top of crocheted strip. Use pliers to bend prongs into crocheted fabric to secure. Connect a jump ring to bail loop. Connect same jump ring to post earring drop using another jump ring.

tying a lariat

The wonderful thing about lariat-style necklaces like this one and the Tied and True Lariat Necklace (page 99) is that you can wear them so many different ways.

WRAP IT UP

Beginning at the front of the neck, wrap the necklace around the neck, criss-crossing at the back. Then bring the ends to the front and tie once to create a choker effect.

IN THE LOOP

Fold the necklace in half. With the fold at your right, wrap the necklace around the neck, from back to front, then slip ends through fold. Position the fold between the left side and center of the neck.

LONG AND LEAN

Wrap the necklace so ends are at front. Tie ends using an overhand knot halfway down the length.

Illustrations by Sharon Watts

sea breeze

This chunky, multi-strand necklace and coordinating looped fringe earrings feature matte-finish tile beads that have the look of surf-tumbled beach glass.

Twisted Strands Necklace

Finished Measurements
- Length approx 20½"/52cm (excluding ties)
- Width at center approx 2½"/6.5cm

Materials
- 2 balls (each approx 284yd/260m) of DMC Inc. *Cebelia Size 10 Crochet Cotton* (mercerized cotton) in #992 aquamarine
- Size C/2 (2.75mm) crochet hook *or size to obtain gauge*
- Two 16"/40.5cm strands (approx one hundred thirty-five beads per strand) of matte-finish glass tile beads each in clear (A), aqua blue (B), peridot (C), teal (D) and emerald (E)
- Any color sewing thread
- Size 7 or 8 sharps sewing needle

Stitch Glossary

SLB Slide bead next to crochet hook. Make next ch using thread coming from opposite side of bead hole along with 2nd strand of thread.

Gauge
32 ch to 4"/10cm over bead pat st using size C/2 (2.75mm) crochet hook and 2 strands of crochet thread held tog.

Take time to check your gauge.

✽ **Note** Due to the initial length of this necklace (approx 9yd/8.25m), you will need a helper to aid you in doubling the strands the first couple of times.

Necklace
Stringing beads
Using needle and thread technique, string one hundred forty-two beads each of A, B, C, D and E onto one strand of crochet thread as foll: *one A, one B, one C, one D, one E; rep from * until all beads are strung.

Beg bead pat st
Row 1 With 2 strands of crochet thread held tog, ch 4, *SLB, with 2 strands held tog, ch 8; rep from * until one bead rem, end SLB, with 2 strands held tog, ch 4. Fasten off.

Finishing
Join ends of necklace tog to form a ring by tying tails in a firm square knot. Weave in ends.

Ties (make 2)
With 2 strands of crochet thread held tog, ch 20, leaving long tails. Join ch with a sl st in first ch forming a loop. Ch 60. Fasten off. leaving long tails. Using needle and thread technique, string on one each of A, B, C, D and E beads. Make an overhand knot close to last bead. Trim off excess tails ¼"/.6cm from knot.

Assembling necklace
When doubling the strands of the ring, keep the strands even in length and the center of the ring open. With the aid of a helper, double the ring to make four strands. Double the ring again to make eight strands. Double the ring again to make sixteen strands, then double the ring one last time to make thirty-two total strands. On work surface, form the ring into an oval. Slip the loop end of a tie under one end of the oval. Insert the beaded end of the tie through the loop, then pull on end to tighten tie around necklace. Rep at opposite end of oval. Pull necklace taut, then twist four or five times.

Looped Fringe Earrings

Finished Measurement
- Length approx 3¼"/8cm

Materials
- 1 ball (approx 284yd/260m) of DMC Inc. *Cebelia Size 10 Crochet Cotton* (mercerized cotton) in #992 aquamarine
- Size 2 (2.25mm) steel crochet hook
- One pair 19mm Contempo silver-finish post earrings with drops
- Eighteen matte-finish glass tile beads each in clear (A), aqua blue (B), peridot (C) and teal (D)
- Sixteen matte-finish glass tile beads in emerald (E)
- Two 3mm round silver-plated beads
- Two 8mm silver-plated cord caps
- Two 1½"/4cm silver-plated eyepins
- Two 5mm round silver-plated jump rings
- Two chain-nose pliers
- Round-nose pliers
- Wire cutters
- Matching sewing thread
- Size 7 or 8 sharps sewing needle

Stitch Glossary

SLB Slide bead next to crochet hook. Make next ch using thread coming from opposite side of bead hole.

Gauge
Gauge is not important.

Earrings (make 2)
Stringing beads
Using needle and thread technique, string nine each of A, B, C, D and eight of E beads onto crochet thread as foll: *one A, one B, one C, one D, one E; rep from * until all beads are strung.

Beg bead pat st
Ch 3.
Row 1 Sc in 2nd ch from hook and in next ch, *ch 2, SLB; rep from * 10 times more, end ch 2, turn, sc in 2 sc. Turn.
Row 2 Ch 1, sc in 2 sc, *ch 2, SLB; rep from * 10 times more, end ch 2, turn, sc in 2 sc. Turn. Rep row 2 twice more—4 looped fringe. Fasten off.

Finishing
Weave in ends.
Forming fringe
Roll the top edge of the fringe into a tight coil. Using sewing needle and matching thread, and working through all layers, sew coil to secure it, taking care that the top of the fringe remains flat.

Attaching cord caps
For each earring, open loop end of an eyepin. Insert shaft of eyepin through center top of crocheted fringe. Draw eyepin through, hooking the crocheted fabric with the open loop. Close the loop, securing the eyepin to the fabric. Thread on a cord cap, then a 3mm bead. Form end of eyepin into a loop.

Assembling earrings
For each earring, connect crocheted fringe to earring drop with a jump ring.

If you prefer the look of gold, simply switch the silver-plated jewelry findings for gold-plated.

tumbling leaves

Dainty glass leaves add dazzle to this super-easy slip-stitch cord necklace. Make it a set with dangling leaf-motif earrings crafted using crochet cotton and gold wire and accented with glass leaves.

Slip-Stitch Cord Necklace

Finished Measurements

- Length approx 21"/53.5cm (including clasp; excluding tassel)
- Width of strap approx ⅜"/1cm

Materials

- 1 ball (approx 284yd/260m) of DMC Inc. *Cebelia Size 10 Crochet Cotton* (mercerized cotton) in #524 very light fern green
- Size C/2 (2.75mm) steel crochet hook *or size to obtain gauge*
- Two 25g packages (approx twenty-seven leaves per package—three large, eight medium and sixteen small) of A Touch of Glass mix glass leaf beads in celery
- One 1"/25mm brass ring
- Two 8mm gold-plated cord caps
- Two 1½"/4cm gold-plated eyepins
- One 12 x 7mm round gold-plated lobster-claw clasp
- Twenty-four 5mm round gold-plated jump rings
- Two chain-nose pliers
- Round-nose pliers
- Wire cutters

Gauge

32 sts to 4"/10cm over sl st using size C/2 (2.75mm) crochet hook and 2 strands of crochet thread held tog.

Take time to check your gauge.

✽ **Note** Wind crochet thread into 2 separate balls and use 2 strands of crochet thread held tog throughout.

Necklace

Right strap

With 2 strands of crochet thread held tog, ch 175.

Turn to bottom lps of ch.

Row 1 Sl st in 2nd bottom lp from hook and in each bottom lp across—174 sts. Fasten off.

Left strap

Work as for right strap.

Tassel

With 2 strands of crochet thread held tog, ch 75.

Turn to bottom lps of ch.

Row 1 Sl st in 2nd bottom lp from hook and in each bottom lp across—74 sts. Fasten off.

Finishing

Weave in ends. Press straps and tassel using a damp pressing cloth.

Attaching cord caps

Fold right strap in half, ends even. Open loop end of an eyepin. Insert shaft of eyepin through center of each end of strap. Draw eyepin through, hooking the ends with the open loop. Close the loop, securing the eyepin to the ends. Thread on a cord cap. Form end of eyepin into a loop. Attach cord cap to left strap as for right.

Assembling necklace

Connect lobster-claw clasp to right strap loop with a jump ring. Connect a jump ring to left strap loop. Insert folded end of right strap through brass ring and draw end through. Insert opposite end with clasp through folded end and pull to tighten half-hitch knot that's formed. Rep for left strap. Fold tassel in half and attach to brass ring in the same manner.

Adding leaves

To make all the wire loops of the leaves the same size, use round-nose pliers to unbend the wire. Use wire cutters to trim the wire leaving ⅜"/1cm extending beyond the top of the leaf. Using round-nose pliers, hold the end of the wire, then bend it into a loop by wrapping it around the top jaw of the pliers until loop is closed. If loop is not centered, adjust its position with chain-nose pliers. Referring to photo for suggested placement, connect five small leaves to each strap using jump rings. For each end of tassel, connect three large leaves, one medium leaf and two small leaves using jump rings.

Leaf-Motif Earrings

Finished Measurement
- Length approx 3⅞"/9.5cm

Materials
- 1 ball (approx 284yd/260m) of DMC Inc. *Cebelia Size 10 Crochet Cotton* (mercerized cotton) in #524 very light fern green
- One spool 34-gauge gold-colored super-fine beading wire
- Six small leaves left over from necklace or one 25g package of A Touch of Glass mix glass leaf beads in celery
- Size C/2 (2.75mm) steel crochet hook *or size to obtain gauge*
- One pair gold-filled French hoop earwires
- One 12"/30.5cm length of gold-plated small drawn cable chain
- Six 8 x 3mm gold-plated prong bails
- Two 5mm round gold-plated jump rings
- Eighteen 4mm round gold-plated jump rings
- Two chain-nose pliers
- Round-nose pliers
- Wire cutters

Gauge
Leaf motif to ⅝" x 1⅛"/2cm x 3cm using size C/2 (2.75mm) crochet hook using 1 strand of crochet thread and 1 strand of wire held tog.

Take time to check gauge.

✱ **Note** Use 1 strand of crochet thread and 1 strand of wire held tog throughout.

Earrings (make 2)
Leaves (make 3)
With 1 strand of crochet thread and 1 strand of wire held tog, ch 6.

Rnd 1 (RS) Work sc in 2nd ch from hook, hdc in next ch, dc in next 2 ch, work 3 dc in last ch, turn to bottom lps of ch, work 3 dc in first lp, dc in next 2 lps, hdc in next lp, sc in last lp, join rnd with a sl st in top of first sc. Fasten off.

Finishing
Weave in ends.
Assembling right earring
Cut three lengths of chain as foll: 4-link (approx ¾"/2cm), 7-link (approx 1¼"/3cm) and 9-link (approx 1⅝"/4cm). For each leaf, position a bail over joining of rnd. Use pliers to bend prongs into crocheted fabric to secure. Attach 4mm jump ring to bail. Use another 4mm jump ring to attach jump ring on bail to chain. With RS of each leaf facing, thread 4-link chain, 9-link chain, then 7-link chain onto a 5mm jump ring; close jump ring. Open earwire drop to connect 5mm jump ring, making sure that RS of leaves face out.

Assembling left earring
Work as for right earring to threading chains onto jump ring. With RS of each leaf facing, thread 7-link chain, 9-link chain, then 4-link chain onto a 5mm jump ring; close jump ring. Connect 5mm jump ring to earwire drop as for right earring.

Adding glass leaves
Make all the wire loops the same size as for necklace. With RS of each leaf facing, use 4mm jump ring to connect leaf to prong bail.

easy weaving

Colorful woven beads combine in an ensemble of dangling ball earrings and a playful rope necklace. Vivid shades of pearl cotton combine beautifully with bright gold findings.

Multicolor Necklace

Finished Measurements
- Length before final assembly approx 47"/119.5cm
- Width approx 1"/2.5cm

Materials
- 1 skein (each approx 7.3yd/25m) each of DMC Inc. *Size 5 Pearl Cotton* (cotton) in #208 very dark lavender, #603 cranberry, #718 plum, #742 light tangerine, #792 dark cornflower blue, #892 medium carnation, #907 light parrot green, #973 bright canary, #995 dark electric blue and #3814 aquamarine
- Size 2 (2.25mm) steel crochet hook *or size to obtain gauge*
- Eleven 20mm round unfinished wooden ball beads with holes
- Twenty-two 6mm round gold-plated corrugated beads
- Twenty-two 10mm gold-plated disc beads
- Eleven 1½"/4cm gold-plated eyepins
- Thirty 5mm gold-plated jump rings
- 54"/137cm length of 3.1mm gold-plated curb chain
- Two chain-nose pliers
- Round-nose pliers
- Wire cutters
- Two small safety pins
- Size 26 chenille needle
- Size 26 tapestry needle

Gauge
Work rnds 1–11 of bead covering using size 2 (2.25mm) steel crochet hook. Insert wooden bead into covering. The covering should fit snugly, but not so tightly that the sts are overstretched. The covering should also cover about two-thirds of the bead. Adjust steel crochet hook size if necessary.

Take time to check your gauge.

Necklace

Bead covering (make 11)
Make 3 using #995 for MC and #907 for CC. Make 2 each using #792 for MC and #603 CC; #208 for MC and #892 for CC; #718 for MC and #742 for CC; and #3814 for MC and #973 CC.

With MC, ch 3. Join ch with a sl st forming a ring.

Rnd 1 Ch 1, work 6 sc in ring. Mark last st made with the safety pin. You will be working in a spiral marking the last st made with a safety pin to indicate end of rnd.

Rnd 2 [Work 2 sc in next st] 6 times—12 sts.

Rnd 3 [Work 2 sc in next st] 12 times—24 sts.

Rnds 4–11 Sc in each st around. When rnd 11 is completed, place lp on hook onto a safety pin.

Beg weaving
Turn bead covering WS out. Thread tail into chenille needle. Weave in tail; trim off excess. Cut a 40"/101.5cm length of CC. Thread into chenille needle. Secure CC with a backstitch to rnd 1. Remove chenille needle, then thread into tapestry needle for weaving. Turn bead covering RS out. From WS, insert needle between first and 2nd sts of rnd 1; draw needle through. From RS, use needle to weave CC over and under sts through rnd 10. Insert wooden bead into covering, matching up hole in bead with center hole of rnd 1. To align the two holes, insert the crochet hook into the wooden bead, then into the covering so it exits the hole. Bring covering up sides of bead. Place loop on safety pin back on crochet hook. Remove safety pin rnd marker. Working into sts with covering on bead, cont to work as foll:

Stitch Glossary

sc2tog [Insert hook in next st, yo and draw up a lp] twice, yo and draw through all 3 lps on hook.

Rnd 12 [Sc2tog] 12 times—12 sts.

Rnd 13 [Sc2tog] 6 times—6 sts.

Rnd 14 [Sc2tog] 3 times—3 sts. Fasten off.

Resume weaving to top of bead.

Finishing

Weave in ends.

Assembling woven beads

Onto each eyepin, thread a 6mm bead, 10mm disc, woven bead, another 10mm disc and 6mm bead. Form end of eyepin into a loop.

Assembling necklace

Cut thirty-eight 12-link (approx 1⅜"/3.5cm) lengths of chain. When connecting pairs of chain, take care that the links of all chain segments face the same direction and are not twisted. For back neck connecting chain, connect nine pairs of chain together using jump rings. Use jump rings to connect the chain pairs together to make a continuous chain; set aside. Refer to photo for suggested color placement or use your own color scheme. Use jump rings to connect woven beads together with pairs of chain. Connect the first and last beads to the connecting chain.

Dangling Ball Earrings

Finished Measurements
• Length approx 2½"/6.5cm

Materials
• 1 skein (each approx 7.3yd/25m) each of DMC Inc. *Size 5 Pearl Cotton* (cotton) in #718 plum (MC) and #742 light tangerine (CC)
• Size 2 (2.25mm) steel crochet hook *or size to obtain gauge*
• Two 16mm round wooden beads
• One pair 8mm half-ball gold-plated earstuds with drops
• Two gold-plated barrel earnuts
• Four 6mm round gold-plated corrugated beads
• Four 10mm gold-plated disc beads
• Two 1½"/4cm gold-plated headpins
• Two 5mm gold-plated jump rings
• 2¼"/5.5cm length of 3.1mm gold-plated curb chain
• Two chain-nose pliers

Stitch Glossary
sc2tog [Insert hook in next st, yo and draw up a lp] twice, yo and draw through all 3 lps on hook.

• Round-nose pliers
• Wire cutters
• Two small safety pins
• Size 26 chenille needle
• Size 26 tapestry needle

Gauge
Work rnds 1–8 of bead covering using size 2 (2.25mm) steel crochet hook. Insert wooden bead into covering. The covering should fit snugly, but not so tightly that the sts are overstretched. The covering should also cover about two-thirds of the bead. Adjust steel crochet hook size if necessary.
Take time to check your gauge.

Earrings (make 2)
Bead covering
With MC, ch 3. Join ch with a sl st forming a ring.
Rnd 1 Ch 1, work 6 sc in ring. Mark last st made with the safety pin. You will be working in a spiral marking the last st made with a safety pin to indicate end of rnd.
Rnd 2 [Work 2 sc in next st] 6 times—12 sts.
Rnd 3 [Work 2 sc in next st, sc in next st] 6 times—18 sts.
Rnds 4–8 Sc in each st around. When rnd 8 is completed, place lp on hook onto a safety pin.

Beg weaving
Turn bead covering WS out. Thread tail into chenille needle. Weave in tail; trim off excess. Cut a 40"/101.5cm length of CC. Thread into chenille needle. Secure CC with a backstitch to rnd 1. Remove chenille needle, then thread into tapestry needle for weaving. Turn bead covering RS out. From WS, insert needle between 1st and 2nd sts of rnd 1; draw needle through. From RS, use needle to weave CC over and under sts through rnd 7. Insert wooden bead into covering, matching up hole in bead with center hole of rnd 1. To align the two holes, insert the crochet hook into the wooden bead, then into the covering so it exits the hole. Bring covering up sides of bead. Place loop on safety pin back on crochet hook. Remove safety pin rnd marker. Working into sts with covering on bead, cont to work as foll:
Rnd 9 [Sc2tog, sc in next st] 6 times—12 sts.
Rnd 10 [Sc2tog] 6 times—6 sts.
Rnd 11 [Sc2tog] 3 times—3 sts. Fasten off.
Resume weaving to top of bead.

Finishing
Weave in ends.
Assembling earrings
For each earring, cut a 7-link (approx ⅞"/2cm) length of chain. Onto a headpin, thread a 6mm bead, 10mm disc, woven bead, another 10mm disc and another 6mm bead. Form end of headpin into a loop and connect it to the chain. Connect chain to the earring drop using a jump ring.

midnight sparkle

This dramatically elegant torque choker features a solitary Irish rose in velvety chenille yarn mounted on a neckwire and studded with a dazzling rhinestone button. A rhinestone buckle and rhinestone button closure add sparkle to the coordinating shirred cuff bracelet.

Irish Rose Choker

Finished Measurements
Irish Rose
- Diameter approx 3½"/9cm

Neckwire
- Diameter approx 5"/12.5cm; inner circumference approx 15¾"/40cm

Materials
- 1 1¾oz/50g hank (approx 98yd/90m) of Crystal Palace Yarns *Cotton Chenille* (combed cotton (5)) in #9598 black
- Size G/6 (4mm) crochet hook *or size to obtain gauge*
- One ⅞"/22m silver-tone rhinestone button
- One 5"/12.5mm silver-plated twisted neckwire with 7.5mm screw-on ball ends
- Matching sewing thread
- Size 7 or 8 sharps sewing needle

Gauge
Irish rose measures approx 3½"/9cm wide using size G/6 (4mm) crochet hook.

Take time to check your gauge.

Irish Rose
To make an adjustable ring, make a slip knot 8"/20.5cm from free end of yarn. Place slip knot on hook, then wrap free end of yarn twice around the first and second fingers of your left hand. Now work from yarn coming from ball as follows:

Rnd 1 (RS) Work 10 sc into ring, pull free end of yarn to close circle, then join rnd with a sl st in first sc.

Rnd 2 Ch 1, work 2 sc in each st around, join rnd with a sl st in first sc—20 sc.

First row of petals
Rnd 3 *Ch 4, sk next 3 sts, sc in next st; rep from * around 5 times—5 ch-4 lps.

Rnd 4 *Work (sc, hdc, dc, 3 tr, dc, hdc, sc) in next ch-4 lp; rep from * around 5 times, join rnd with a sl st in first sc—5 petals made. Fasten off.

Second row of petals
With RS facing, fold first row of petals toward you, join yarn with a sl st in 2nd st of any of the 3 skipped sts of rnd 3.

Rnd 5 *Ch 5, sk next 3 sts of rnd 3, sl st in next st; rep from * around 4 times, end ch 5, sk next 3 sts, join rnd with a sl st in first sl st—5 ch-5 lps.

Rnd 6 *Work (hdc, 2 dc, 5 tr, 2 dc, hdc) in next ch-5 lp; rep from * around 5 times—5 petals made, join rnd with a sl st in first hdc. Fasten off.

Finishing
Weave in ends. Using thread doubled in sewing needle, sew button to center of rose. Sew rose securely to the neckwire.

Velvety Cuff Bracelet

Finished Measurements
- Circumference (fastened) approx 6½"/16.5cm
- Width approx 3¼"/8cm

Materials
- 1 1¾oz/50g hank (approx 98yd/90m) of Crystal Palace Yarns *Cotton Chenille* (combed cotton (**5**)) in #9598 black
- Size G/6 (4mm) crochet hook *or size to obtain gauge*
- One 1½" x 1⅞"/38mm x 47mm oval silver-tone rhinestone buckle
- Two ⅝"/16mm silver-tone rhinestone buttons
- Matching sewing thread
- Size 7 or 8 sharps sewing needle

Gauge
10 sts to 3"/7.5cm and 5 rows to 4"/10cm over tr using size G/6 (4mm) crochet hook.
Take time to check your gauge.

Stitch Glossary
tr2tog [Yo twice, insert hook in next st, yo and draw up a lp, (yo, draw through 2 lps on hook) twice] twice, yo and draw through all 3 lps on hook.

Cuff Bracelet
Ch 7.

Row 1 Sc in 2nd ch from hook and in each ch across—6 sts. Turn.

Rows 2–4 Ch 1, sc in each st across. Turn.

Row 5 Ch 4, work 2 tr in each st across—12 sts. Turn.

Rows 6–10 Ch 4, sk first st, tr in next 11 sts, end tr in top of t-ch of row below. Turn.

Row 11 Ch 4, sk first st, [tr2tog] 5 times, end tr2tog over last st and top of t-ch of row below—6 sts. Turn.

Row 12 Ch 1, sc in each st across. Turn.

Row (buttonhole) 13 Ch 1, sc in first st, ch 2, sk next st, sc in next 2 sts, ch 2, sk next st, sc in last st. Turn.

Row 14 Ch 1, sc in each st across, working 2 sc over each ch-2 sp. Fasten off.

Finishing
Weave in ends. Thread bracelet through buckle, centering 4th tr row in buckle opening. Distribute gathers evenly in opening. Using thread doubled in sewing needle, sew on buttons to correspond to buttonholes.

Glittery rhinestone accents evoke the glamour of the *Great Gatsby* era.

victorian elegance

Pretty pearls make this lovely suite suitable for a bride. The choker and the crocheted bead earrings feature teardrop pearls, while two different-size round pearls highlight the bracelet's spiral design.

Teardrop Choker

Finished Measurements
- Length approx 13½"/34cm (including clasp and chain; adjustable to 17"/43cm)
- Width approx 1⅝"/4cm (excluding drop pearls)

Materials
- 1 ball (approx 284yd/260m) of DMC Inc. *Cebelia Size 10 Crochet Cotton* (mercerized cotton) in #712 cream
- Size 2 (2.25mm) steel crochet hook *or size to obtain gauge*
- Two hundred thirty-four 4mm round cultura pearls
- Twenty-nine 6 x 12mm drop cultura pearls with wire
- Fourteen 9 x 20mm drop cultura pearls with wire
- One set antique gold cast-pewter floral three-hole end bar with chain and lobster-claw clasp
- One 5mm round gold-plated jump ring

Stitch Glossary
SLP Slide round pearl next to crochet hook.
SLD Slide drop pearl next to crochet hook.

- Two chain-nose pliers
- Matching sewing thread
- Size 7 or 8 sharps sewing needle

Gauge
38 sts to 4"/10cm and 6 rows to ½"/1.3cm over bead pat st using size 2 (2.25mm) crochet hook.
Take time to check your gauge.

Choker
Stringing beads
Using needle and thread technique, string drop pearls and round pearls onto crochet thread as foll: [one small drop, one large drop, one small drop] 14 times, then string on all round pearls.

Beg bead pat st
Ch 114.

Row 1 (RS) Sc in 2nd ch from hook and in each ch across—113 sts. Ch 1, turn.

Row 2 Sc in first st, *SLP, sc in next 2 sts; rep from * to end. Ch 1, turn.

Row 3 Sc in each st across. Ch 1, turn.

Row 4 Sc in first 2 sts, *SLP, sc in next 2 sts; rep from *, end SLP, sc in last st. Ch 1, turn.

Row 5 Rep row 3.

Row 6 Rep row 2.

Row 7 Rep row 3.

Row 8 Sc in first st, [SLP, sc in next st] twice, *ch 9, sk next 3 sts, sc in next st, [SLP, sc in next st] 3 times, sc in next st; rep from *, end ch 9, sk next 3 sts, sc in next st, [SLP, sc in next st] twice. Ch 1, turn.

Row 9 Sc in first 2 sts, *ch 5, sc in ch-9 lp, ch 5, sk next sc, sc in next 3 sts; rep from *, end last rep sc in last 2 sc. Ch 1, turn.

Row 10 Sc in first sc, *ch 5, SLP, sc in next sc, ch 5, sk next sc, SLP, sc in next sc; rep from *, end ch 5, sk next sc, SLP, sc in last sc. Ch 1, turn.

Row 11 Sc in first sc, *ch 5, sl st in next sc, [ch 4, SLD, ch 4, sl st in same sc as last sl st] 3 times, ch 5, sc in next sc; rep from * to end. Fasten off.

Finishing

Weave in ends. With RS facing, position lobster-claw end bar at right end of choker. Have top edge of end bar even with top edge of choker. Sew securely using needle and thread. Rep for chain end bar and left end of necklace. Connect rem small drop pearl to end of chain with jump ring.

Chandelier Earrings

Finished Measurement
• Length approx 2½"/6.5cm

Materials
• 1 ball (approx 284yd/260m) of DMC Inc. *Cebelia Size 10 Crochet Cotton* (mercerized cotton) in #712 cream
• Size 2 (2.25mm) steel crochet hook
• Two 18 x 10mm oval wooden beads in white
• One pair antique gold post earrings with three-loop chandelier drops
• Four 6 x 12mm drop cultura pearls with wire
• Four 4mm round cultura pearls
• Two 3mm round cultura pearls
• Four 10mm antique gold cast-pewter bead caps
• Four 6mm antique gold cast-pewter bead caps
• Six 4mm round gold-plated jump rings
• Two 1½"/4cm gold-plated headpins
• Two chain-nose pliers
• Round-nose pliers
• Wire cutters
• Small safety pin

Gauge
Gauge is not important.

Stitch Glossary

sc2tog [Insert hook in next st, yo and draw up a lp] twice, yo and draw through all 3 lps on hook.

Earrings (make 2)
Covering bead
Ch 3. Join ch with a sl st forming a ring.

Rnd 1 (RS) Ch 1, work 6 sc in ring. Mark last st made with the safety pin. You will be working in a spiral marking the last st made with the safety pin to indicate end of rnd.

Rnd 2 [Sc in next st, work 2 sc in next st] 3 times—9 sts.

Rnd 3 [Sc in next 2 sts, work 2 sc in next st] 3 times—12 sts.

Rnd 4 [Sc in next 3 sts, work 2 sc in next st] 3 times—15 sts.

Rnds 5–9 Sc in each st around. When rnd 9 is completed, insert wooden bead into covering, matching up hole in bead with center hole of rnd 1. To align the two holes, insert the crochet hook into the wooden bead, then into the covering so it exits the hole. Bring covering up sides of bead; remove safety pin. Working into sts with covering on bead, cont to work as foll:

Rnd 10 [Sc in next 3 sts, sc2tog] 3 times—12 sts.

Rnd 11 [Sc2tog] 6 times—6 sts.

Rnd 12 [Sc2tog] 3 times—3 sts. Fasten off.

Finishing
Weave in ends.
Assembling crocheted beads
Onto a headpin, thread a 3mm pearl, 4mm pearl, 10mm bead cap, crocheted bead, 10mm bead cap and a 4mm pearl. Form end of headpin into a loop.
Assembling drop pearls
For each drop pearl, open wire loop first, then straighten wire. Thread a 6mm bead cap onto wire; reform loop using round-nose pliers.
Assembling earrings
For each earring, use a jump ring to connect a crocheted bead assembly to center loop of chandelier drop. Use jump rings to connect a drop pearl assembly to right loop and left loop of chandelier drop.

Pearl Twist Bracelet

Finished Measurements
- Length approx 8⅝"/22cm (including toggle clasp)
- Width approx 1¾"/4.5cm

Materials
- 1 ball (approx 284yd/260m) of DMC Inc. *Cebelia Size 10 Crochet Cotton* (mercerized cotton) in #712 cream
- Size C/2 (2.75mm) crochet hook *or size to obtain gauge*
- One hundred sixty-six 4mm round cultura pearls
- Seventy-eight 6mm round cultura pearls
- Two 3mm round gold-plated corrugated beads
- Two 10mm x 7mm antique gold cast-pewter floral cones
- Two 1½"/4cm gold-plated eyepins
- One 18mm x 12mm antique gold cast-pewter floral bar-and-ring toggle clasp
- Chain-nose pliers
- Round-nose pliers
- Wire cutters
- Matching sewing thread
- Size 7 or 8 sharps sewing needle

Stitch Glossary

SLP Slide pearl next to crochet hook.

sc2tog [Insert hook in next st, yo and draw up a lp] twice, yo and draw through all 3 lps on hook.

Gauge
6 sts to ¾"/2cm diameter and 24 rnds to 4"/10cm over tubular crochet using size C/2 (2.75mm) crochet hook.

Take time to check your gauge.

Bracelet

Stringing pearls
Using needle and thread technique, string pearls onto crochet thread as foll: six 4mm, *one 6mm, two 4mm; rep from * until all pearls are strung.

Tubular crochet
Ch 3. Join ch with a sl st forming a ring.

Rnd 1 Work 6 sc in ring. Do not join. You will be working in a spiral where rnds are not joined.

Rnd 2 [Insert hook in next st, SLP, yo and draw up a lp, yo and draw through both lps on hook] 6 times. You will now be working from the WS.

Rnd 3 [Insert hook under horizontal thread coming out of RH side of next pearl of rnd below, SLP, yo and draw up a lp, yo and draw through both lps on hook] 6 times. Rep rnd 3 for tubular crochet and work until all pearls are used.

Next rnd [Insert hook under horizontal thread coming out of RH side of next pearl of rnd below, yo and draw up a lp, yo and draw through both lps on hook] 6 times.

Last rnd [Sc2tog] 3 times. Fasten off.

Finishing
Weave in ends.

Assembling bracelet
Open loop end of an eyepin. Insert shaft of eyepin through center of one end of crocheted tube. Draw eyepin through, hooking the crocheted fabric with the open loop. Close the loop, securing the eyepin to the fabric. Thread on a floral cone and a corrugated bead. Form end of eyepin into a loop connecting it to ring portion of toggle clasp. Working in the same manner, attach floral cone along with a corrugated bead to opposite end of crocheted tube. Connect eyepin loop to bar portion of toggle clasp.

Elegant oval crocheted bead earrings feature dainty teardrop pearls that echo those on the necklace.

forever roses

The classic Irish rose gets a whole new look when edged with tiny glass beads. Small roses become beautiful button earrings, while one large rose creates the focal point for a multi-strand beaded necklace.

Multi-Strand Rose Necklace

Finished Measurements
- Length approx 21"/53.5cm (including clasp)

Beaded Strands
- Width approx ⅝"/1.6cm

Irish Rose
- Diameter approx 1⅞"/4.5cm

Materials
- 1 ball (approx 284yd/260m) of DMC Inc. *Cebelia Size 10 Crochet Cotton* (mercerized cotton) in #223 medium shell pink
- Size 2 (2.25mm) steel crochet hook *or size to obtain gauge*
- Three 16"/40.5cm strands (approx one hundred thirty-six beads per strand) of 3mm round Czech glass lustre beads in pink
- Two 16"/40.5cm strands (approx sixty-seven beads per strand) of 6mm round Czech glass lustre beads in pink
- One 16"/40.5cm strand (approx fifty beads per strand) of 8mm round Czech glass lustre beads in pink
- Six gold-plated crimp beads
- Six 5mm round gold-plated jump rings
- One gold-plated three-loop hook-style clasp
- One 1"/25mm-diameter plastic circle (cut from a container lid)
- Crimping pliers (optional)
- Two chain-nose pliers
- Matching sewing thread
- Size 7 or 8 sharps sewing needle
- Small safety pin

Gauge
Irish rose measures 1⅞"/4.5cm wide using size 2 (2.25mm) steel crochet hook.

Take time to check your gauge.

Necklace
Irish Rose

Stringing beads for first row of petals
Using needle and thread technique, string forty 3mm beads onto crochet thread.

First row of petals
Ch 5. Join ch with a sl st forming a ring.

Rnd 1 (RS) Ch 1, work 10 sc into ring, join rnd with a sl st in first st.

Rnd 2 Ch 1, work 2 sc in each st around, join rnd with a sl st in first st—20 sts.

Rnd 3 *Ch 4, sk next 3 sts, sc in next st; rep from * around 4 times more—5 ch-4 lps.

Rnd 4 *Work (sc SLB, hdc SLB, dc SLB, [tr, SLB] 3 times, dc SLB, hdc SLB, sc) in next ch-4 lp; rep from * around 4 times more, join rnd with a sl st in first st—5 petals made. Fasten off. Weave in ends.

Stringing beads for second row of petals
Using needle and thread technique, string fifty 3mm beads onto crochet thread.

Second row of petals
With RS facing, fold first row of petals towards you. Join yarn with a sl st in 2nd st of any of the 3 skipped sts of rnd 3.

Rnd 5 *Ch 5, sk next 3 sts of rnd 3, sl st in next st; rep from * around 3 times more, end ch 5, sk next 3 sts, join rnd with a sl st in first st—5 ch-5 lps.

Rnd 6 *Work (hdc SLB, [dc, SLB] twice, [tr, SLB] 5 times, [dc, SLB] twice, hdc) in next ch-5 lp; rep from * around 4 times more, join rnd with a sl st in first st—5 petals made. Fasten off. Weave in ends.

Stitch Glossary

SLB Slide bead next to crochet hook.

dtr (double treble crochet) Yo 3 times, insert hook into ch-lp, yo and draw up a lp, [yo and draw through 2 lps on hook] 4 times.

Stringing beads for third row of petals

Using needle and thread technique, string sixty 3mm beads onto crochet thread.

Third row of petals

With RS facing, fold first and second rows of petals toward you. Join yarn with a sl st around post of sc of rnd 3.

Rnd 7 *Ch 6, sl st around post of next sc of rnd 3; rep from * around 3 times more, end ch 6, join rnd with a sl st in first sl st—5 ch-6 lps.

Rnd 8 *Work ([dc, SLB] twice, [tr, SLB] 3 times, [dtr, SLB] 3 times, [tr, SLB] 3 times, dc, SLB, dc) in next ch-6 lp; rep from * around 4 times more, join rnd with a sl st in first st—5 petals made. Fasten off.

Backing

Ch 3. Join ch with a sl st forming a ring.

Rnd 1 (RS) Work 6 sc in ring. Mark last st made with the safety pin. You will be working in a spiral, marking the last st made with the safety pin to indicate end of rnd.

Rnd 2 Work 2 sc in each st around—12 sts.

Rnd 3 [Sc in next st, work 2 sc in next st] 6 times—18 sts.

Rnd 4 [Sc in next 2 sts, work 2 sc in next st] 6 times—24 sts.

Rnd 5 [Sc in next 3 sts, work 2 sc in next st] 6 times—30 sts.

Rnd 6 [Sc in next 4 sts, work 2 sc in next st] 6 times—36 sts. Fasten off, leaving a long tail for sewing.

Finishing

Weave in rem ends. Sew one 8mm bead securely to center of rose using sewing needle and thread. With WS facing, position backing on center back of rose. Using backing tail, whipstitch edge of backing to rose leaving a 1"/2.5cm opening. Insert plastic circle; whipstitch opening closed.

Stringing necklace

For first (top) strand of beads, cut a 32"/81cm length of crochet thread. Thread into tapestry needle. With RS of rose facing, position rose so one of the third-row petals is at center top. Flip rose over to WS so this petal is at top. Working from right to left, insert tapestry needle through backing/rose seam, approx ⅜"/1cm from tip of top petal. Draw needle through backing and even up ends. For RH strand of crochet thread, use needle and thread technique to string on twenty-nine 3mm beads and twenty-eight 6mm beads as foll: string on a 3mm bead, then alternate 6mm and 3mm beads to the end. Continuing to use needle and thread technique, thread on a crimp bead, then a jump ring. Skip the jump ring, then insert needle back through crimp bead and first four beads. Remove needle and thread. Pull on tail to remove slack. Use crimping pliers to crimp bead. Trim excess crochet thread close to bead hole. Rep for LH strand of crochet thread.

For second (center) strand of beads, cut a 36"/91.5cm length of crochet thread. Thread into tapestry needle. With WS of rose facing, insert tapestry needle through backing/rose seam, approx ¼"/.6cm below first strand. Draw needle through backing and even up ends. For RH strand of crochet thread, use needle and thread technique to string on two 3mm beads, eighteen 6mm beads and seventeen 8mm beads as foll: string on a 6mm bead, then alternate 8mm and 6mm beads to the end, then string on the two 3mm beads. Finish with a crimp bead and jump ring as for first strand. Rep for LH strand of crochet thread.

For third (bottom) strand of beads, cut a 38"/96.5cm length of crochet thread. Thread into tapestry needle. With WS of rose facing, insert tapestry needle through backing/rose seam, approx ¼"/.6cm below second strand. Draw needle through backing and even up ends. For RH strand of crochet thread, use needle and thread technique to string on thirty-one 3mm beads and thirty 6mm beads as foll: string on a 3mm bead, then alternate 6mm and 3mm beads to the end. Finish with a crimp bead and jump ring as for first strand. Rep for LH strand of crochet thread.

Assembling necklace

Taking care not to twist bead strands, connect RH strands to hook portion of clasp with jump rings attached to strands. Connect LH strands of beads to loop portion of clasp with jump rings attached to strands.

Button Earrings

Finished Measurement

Diameter approx 1⅛"/3cm

Materials

- 1 ball (approx 284yd/260m) of DMC Inc. *Cebelia Size 10 Crochet Cotton* (mercerized cotton) in #223 medium shell pink
- Size 2 (2.25mm) steel crochet hook *or size to obtain gauge*
- Eighteen 3mm round Czech glass lustre beads in pink
- Two 6mm round Czech glass lustre beads in pink
- One pair 4mm round gold-plated flat pad earstuds
- One pair gold-plated earnuts

- Bond 527 multi-purpose cement or other clear, permanent adhesive
- Medium-grit sandpaper or emery board
- Paper plate
- Matching sewing thread
- Size 7 or 8 sharps sewing needle

Gauge

Rose measures 1⅛"/3cm wide using size 2 (2.25mm) steel crochet hook.

Take time to check your gauge.

Earrings (make 2)

Rose

Ch 5. Join ch with a sl st forming a ring.

First row of petals

Rnd 1 (RS) Ch 1, work 15 sc into ring, join rnd with a sl st in first st.

Rnd 2 *Ch 4, sk next 2 sts, sc in next st; rep from * around 4 times more—5 ch-4 lps.

Rnd 3 *Work (sc, 3 dc, tr, 3 dc, sc) in next ch-4 lp; rep from * around 4 times more, join rnd with a sl st in first st—5 petals made. Fasten off.

Second row of petals

With RS facing, fold first row of petals toward you. Join yarn with a sl st in 2nd st of any of the 2 skipped sts of rnd 1.

Rnd 4 *Ch 5, sk next 2 sts of rnd 1, sl st in next st; rep from * around 3 times more, end ch 5, sk next 2 sts, join rnd with a sl st in joining sl st—5 ch-5 lps.

Rnd 6 *Work (sc, 2 dc, 4 tr, 2 dc, sc) in next ch-5 lp; rep from * around 4 times more, join rnd with a sl st in first st—5 petals made. Fasten off.

Finishing

Weave in ends. For each earring, sew one 6mm bead securely to center of a rose using sewing needle and thread. Thread needle with a strand of thread and knot end. Working from WS to RS, insert needle in center of space between 6mm bead and rnd 2. String on nine 3mm beads. Wrap strand of 3mm beads around 6mm bead. Working from RS to WS, insert needle in same place it exited and draw through. To secure ring of 3mm beads, stitch over thread strand between every bead around. Fasten off thread securely.

Assembling earrings

For each earring, use sandpaper or emery board to roughen the surface of an earstud pad. Apply glue to earstud pad. Position rose on earstud pad, then press in place. Place earring upside down on paper plate. Let dry overnight before wearing.

Create a garden of rose lapel pins by sewing on pin backs instead of attaching earstuds.

chain links

Double your accessorizing options by wearing this string-of-rings as a long rope or as a two-strand necklace. Crochet the necklace, matching bracelet and earrings using two dazzling shades of metallic yarn.

Black and Gold Necklace

Finished Measurements

- Length approx 47"/119.5cm (excluding hook)
- Width approx 1¼"/3cm

Materials

- 1 .880oz/25g hank (each approx 85yd/78m) each of Berroco, Inc. *Metallic FX* (rayon/metallic (**3**)) in #1006 black (A) and #1003 gold/black (B)
- Size C/2 (2.75mm) crochet hook
- Fifty-seven 24mm round gold-plated split rings
- One black thread-covered hook-and-eye set (hook ⅞"/22mm long; discard eye)

- Black sewing thread
- Size 7 or 8 sharps sewing needle
- Chain-nose pliers
- Size 26 chenille needle

Gauge

Gauge is not important.

✱ **Note** You will find it helpful to use pliers to pull the chenille needle through when weaving in ends.

Necklace

Connect split rings tog forming a long chain.

Covering ring 1

Rnd 1 (RS) With A, make a slip knot leaving a 4"/10cm tail, then place on hook.

Join A to first ring with a sc. Slide sc to split opening. Making sure to work tightly and evenly, work 32 sc over ring. Bring beg tail to RS. Working over beg tail, work approx 5 sc more, making sure that ring is completely covered and that sts do not overlap. Cut yarn leaving a 6"/15cm tail. Do not fasten off, just draw this end tail through last st. Pull on beg tail to remove slack, then cut off close to sts. Thread end tail in chenille needle. Insert needle into top of first sc, draw yarn through. On WS, weave in end.

Covering ring 2

Using B, work rnd 1 over 2nd ring as for covering ring 1. Cont to cover rings, alternating A and B and making sure that RS of new ring matches RS of previous ring of the same color.

Finishing

Using sewing needle and double strand of thread, sew hook securely to one end of chain.

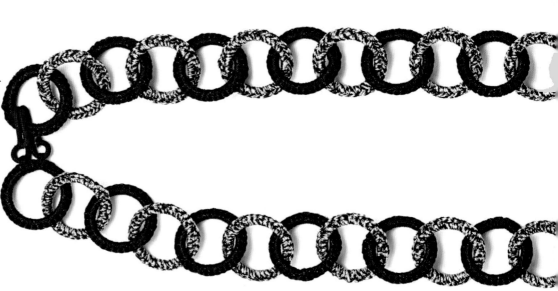

You can also wear this extra-long necklace as a trendy chain belt, either around your waist or low on the hips.

Linked Bracelet

Finished Measurements
- Length approx 8"/20.5cm (including toggle clasp)
- Width approx 1¼"/3cm

Materials
- 1 .8802oz/25g hank (approx 85yd/78m) of Berroco, Inc. *Metallic FX* (rayon/metallic (**3**)) in #1003 gold/black
- Size C/2 (2.75mm) crochet hook
- Five 24mm round gold-plated split rings
- Six 16mm round gold-plated split rings

- Two 6 x 4mm oval gold-plated jump rings
- One 20 x 15mm antique gold cast-pewter bar-and-ring toggle clasp
- Two chain-nose pliers
- Size 26 chenille needle

Gauge
Gauge is not important.

�֎ **Note** You will find it helpful to use pliers to pull the chenille needle through when weaving in ends.

Bracelet
Connect 24mm split rings with 16mm split rings. Connect another 16mm ring to first and last 24mm rings. (**Note** It's important to connect the smaller rings to the larger rings before covering the larger rings with crochet, as you won't be able to connect the smaller rings once the coverings are completed.)

Covering rings
Rnd 1 (RS) Make a slip knot leaving a 4"/10cm tail, then place on hook. Join yarn to the first large split ring with a sc. Slide sc to split opening. Making sure to work tightly and evenly, work 32 sc over ring. Bring beg tail to RS. Working over beg tail, work approx 5 sc more, making sure that ring is completely covered and that sts do not overlap. Cut yarn leaving a 6"/15cm tail. Do not fasten off, just draw this end tail through last st. Pull on beg tail to remove slack, then cut off close to sts. Thread end tail in chenille needle. Insert needle into top of first sc, draw yarn through. On WS, weave in end. Cont to cover rem large rings making sure that all RS are facing the same way.

Finishing
Connect ring portion of toggle clasp to one of the end 16mm split rings. Connect an oval jump ring to 16mm split ring on opposite end. Connect the bar portion of toggle clasp to this oval jump ring with rem oval jump ring.

Dangling Rings Earrings

Finished Measurement

- Length approx 2½"/6.5cm

Materials

- 1 .8802oz/25g hank (approx 85yd/78m) of Berroco, Inc. *Metallic FX* (rayon/metallic (3)) in #1006 black
- Size C/2 (2.75mm) crochet hook
- One pair 19mm Contempo gold-finish post earrings with drops
- Two 24mm round gold-plated split rings
- Four 16mm round gold-plated split rings
- Chain-nose pliers
- Size 26 chenille needle

Gauge

Gauge is not important.

❋ **Note** You will find it helpful to use pliers to pull the chenille needle through when weaving in ends.

Earrings (make 2)

Connect one 16mm split ring to a 24mm split ring.
(**Note** It's important to connect the smaller ring to the larger ring before covering the larger ring with crochet, as you won't be able to connect the smaller ring once the covering is completed.)

Covering ring

Rnd 1 (RS) Make a slip knot leaving a 4"/10cm tail, then place on hook. Join yarn to the large split ring with a sc. Slide sc to split opening. Making sure to work tightly and evenly, work 32 sc over ring. Bring beg tail to RS. Working over beg tail, work approx 5 sc more, making sure that ring is completely covered and that sts do not overlap. Cut yarn leaving a 6"/15cm tail. Do not fasten off, just draw this end tail through last st. Pull on beg tail to remove slack, then cut off close to sts. Thread end tail in chenille needle. Insert needle into top of first sc, draw yarn through. On WS, weave in end.

Finishing

Assembling earrings

For each earring, connect a 16mm ring to the previous 16mm ring. Connect the second 16mm ring to the earring drop, making sure that RS of covered ring faces out.

lovely in lavender

This flattering choker features tiny faceted beads and daggers.
Elegant crocheted oval drop earrings are the perfect companions.

Beaded Choker

Finished Measurements

- Length 14¼"/36cm (including clasp and chain; adjustable to 17½"/44cm)
- Width approx ⅝"/1.5cm (excluding daggers)

Materials

- 1 ball (approx 284yd/260m) of DMC Inc. *Cebelia Size 10 Crochet Cotton* (mercerized cotton) in #210 medium lavender
- Size 2 (2.25mm) steel crochet hook *or size to obtain gauge*
- Two hundred nineteen 4mm round marbled fire-polished glass beads in lavender
- Fifty-two marbled fire-polished glass daggers in lavender
- One set antique silver cast-pewter three-hole end bar with chain and lobster-claw clasp
- One 4mm round silver-plated jump ring

Stitch Glossary

SLB Slide bead next to crochet hook.

SLD Slide dagger next to crochet hook.

- Two chain-nose pliers
- Matching sewing thread
- Size 7 or 8 sharps sewing needle

Gauge

6 sts to ⅝"/1.5cm and 10 rows to 1"/2.5cm over bead pat st using size 2 (2.25mm) steel crochet hook.
Take time to check your gauge.

Choker

Stringing beads

Using needle and thread technique, string beads and daggers onto crochet thread as foll: 9 beads, *[1 dagger, 3 beads] 3 times, 3 beads; rep from * 16 times more, end 6 beads.

Beg bead pat st

Ch 7, leaving a long tail for sewing.

Row 1 Sc in 2nd ch from hook and in each ch across—6 sts. Turn.

Rows 2 and 3 Ch 1, sc in each st across. Turn.

Row 4 (WS) Ch 1, sc in first st, [SLB, sc in next st, sc in following st] twice, SLB, sc in last st. Turn.

Row 5 and all RS rows Ch 1, sc in each st across. Turn.

Row 6 Rep row 4.

Rows 7, 9 and 11 Ch 1, sc in first st, [SLB, sc in next st, sc in following st] twice, SLB, sc in last st, SLD. Turn.

Row 13 Rep row 4.

Row 14 Rep row 5.

Rows 15–142 Rep rows 7–14 16 times more.

Row 143 Rep row 4.

Row 144 Rep row 5.

Row 145 Rep row 4.

Rows 146–148 Rep row 5. Fasten off leaving a long tail for sewing.

Finishing

Fold choker to WS along row 3; sew in place using beg tail. Sew lobster-claw end bar securely to this end using sewing needle and thread. Fold choker to WS along row 146; sew in place using end tail. Sew chain end bar securely to this end using needle and thread. Connect rem dagger to end of chain with jump ring.

Oval Bead Drop Earrings

Finished Measurement
- Length approx 2⅛"/5.5cm

Materials
- 1 ball (approx 284yd/260m) of DMC Inc. *Cebelia Size 10 Crochet Cotton* (mercerized cotton) in #210 medium lavender
- Size 2 (2.25mm) steel crochet
- Two 18 x 10mm oval wooden beads in white
- One pair antique silver post earrings with drops
- Four 4mm round marbled fire-polished glass beads in lavender
- Two 14mm antique silver cast-pewter end caps
- Two 12mm antique silver cast-pewter bead caps
- Two 4mm round silver-plated jump rings
- Two 1½"/4cm silver-plated headpins
- Two chain-nose pliers
- Round-nose pliers
- Wire cutters
- Small safety pin
- Size 26 tapestry needle

Stitch Glossary

sc2tog [Insert hook in next st, yo and draw up a lp] twice, yo and draw through all 3 lps on hook.

Gauge
Gauge is not important.

Earrings (make 2)
Covering bead
Ch 3, leaving a 25"/63.5cm tail for weaving. Join ch with a sl st, forming a ring.

Rnd 1 (RS) Ch 1, work 6 sc in ring. Mark last st made with the safety pin. You will be working in a spiral marking the last st made with the safety pin to indicate end of rnd.

Rnd 2 [Sc in next st, work 2 sc in next st] 3 times—9 sts. Draw tail out through bottom hole to RS (if necessary).

Rnd 3 [Sc in next 2 sts, work 2 sc in next st] 3 times—12 sts.

Rnd 4 [Sc in next 3 sts, work 2 sc in next st] 3 times—15 sts.

Rnds 5 and 6 Sc in each st around.

Beg weaving
Thread tail in tapestry needle. Insert needle back through bottom hole, then insert needle in space between 1st and 2nd sts of rnd 1; draw needle through. From RS, use needle to weave crochet thread over and under sts through rnd 5.

Rnds 7–9 Sc in each st around. When rnd 9 is completed, insert wooden bead into covering, matching up hole in bead with center hole of rnd 1. To align the two holes, insert the crochet hook into the wooden bead, then into the covering so it exits the hole. Bring covering up sides of bead; remove safety pin. Working into sts with covering on bead, cont to work as foll:

Rnd 10 [Sc in next 3 sts, sc2tog] 3 times—12 sts.

Rnd 11 [Sc2tog] 6 times—6 sts.

Rnd 12 [Sc2tog] 3 times—3 sts. Fasten off.
Resume weaving to top of bead.

Finishing
Weave in ends.
Assembling earrings
For each earring, thread a fire-polished bead onto a headpin. Onto same headpin, thread a bead cap, crocheted bead, end cap and another fire-polished bead. Form end of headpin into a loop. Connect crocheted bead assembly to earring drop with a jump ring.

This choker becomes a delightful collar necklace when you wear it more loosely around your neck.

southwest style

The look of Native American adornment is captured in crochet using suede-like yarn. The cross-stitched choker is accented with an authentic abalone disc and red crow beads. Pair it with a matching cuff that fastens with a silver concho button.

Cross-Stitched Choker

Finished Measurements
- Length approx 12½"/ 32cm (excluding ties)
- Width approx 1⅝"/4cm

Materials
- 1 1¾oz/50g ball (each approx 120yd/110m) each of Berroco, Inc. *Suede* (nylon ④) in #3717 wild bill hickock (MC) and #3714 hopalong cassidy (CC)
- Size 7 (4.5mm) crochet hook *or size to obtain gauge*
- One 1½"/40mm two-hole abalone button
- Seven 9mm opaque glass crow beads in red

Gauge
20 sts and 23 rows to 4"/10cm over sc using size 7 (4.5mm) crochet hook.

Take time to check your gauge.

Stitch Glossary

sc2tog [Insert hook in next st, yo and draw up a lp] twice, yo and draw through all 3 lps on hook.

sc3tog [Insert hook in next st, yo and draw up a lp] 3 times, yo and draw through all 4 lps on hook.

Choker

With MC, ch 46 (for tie).

Row 1 (RS) Work 3 sc in 2nd ch from hook. Turn.

Row 2 Ch 1, work 2 sc in first st, sc in next st, work 2 sc in last st—5 sts. Turn.

Row 3 Ch 1, work 2 sc in first st, sc in next 3 sts, work 2 sc in last st—7 sts. Turn.

Rows 4–65 Ch 1, sc in each st across. Turn. Piece should measure approx 12"/30.5cm from beg (not including tie). Turn.

Row 66 Ch 1, sc2tog, sc in next 3 sts, sc2tog—5 sts. Turn.

Row 67 Ch 1, sc2tog, sc in next st, sc2tog—3 sts. Turn.

Row 68 Ch 1, sc3tog—1 st. Ch 45 (for tie). Fasten off.

Finishing

Weave in ends.

Edging
With RS facing, join CC with a sl st in left side edge of row 1. Rnd 1 (RS) Ch 2, working from left to right, *skip next row, hdc in side edge of next row, ch 1; rep from * around, omitting skipping rows as you go around curves so work lies flat, join rnd with a sl st in top of beg ch-2. Fasten off. Weave in ends.

Embroidery
Work chart on the next page using one strand of CC. Work each cross stitch over 2 sts and 2 rows making sure that yarn lies flat. With RS facing, beg chart on rows 9/10, working first cross stitch over sts 3 and 4. (**Note** The ch-1 t-ch at beg of each RS row counts as one st, but is not represented on the chart.) Work chart to row 60. Cut two 16"/40.5cm strands of CC. Thread both strands in tapestry needle. Position button in center of choker, so

buttonholes are vertical. Working from RS to WS, insert needle through bottom hole; draw half the yarn through. Working from WS to RS, insert needle through top hole; draw rem yarn through. Remove needle. Thread yarn ends through a crow bead. Even up yarn ends, removing slack so bead is as close as possible to button. Tie yarn ends in a square knot to secure button and bead in place. For each pair of yarn ends, make an overhand knot 3"/7.5cm from first knot. Thread three crow beads onto end, then make an overhand knot close to bottom of last bead to secure beads in place. Trim yarn ends 1"/2.5cm from last knot.

Cross-Stitched Cuff

Finished Measurements
• Length approx 9½"/ 24cm (excluding button loop) but can be made to fit any wrist size
• Width approx 2½"/6.5cm

Materials
• 1 1¾oz/50g ball (each approx 120yd/110m) each of Berroco, Inc. *Suede* (nylon ) in #3714 hopalong cassidy (MC) and #3717 wild bill hickock (CC)
• Size G/6 (4mm) crochet hook *or size to obtain gauge*
• One ¾"/19mm silver concho button
• One large metal snap

• Matching sewing thread
• Size 7 or 8 sharps sewing needle

Gauge
20 sts and 24 rows to 4"/10cm over sc using size G/6 (4mm) crochet hook.
Take time to check your gauge.

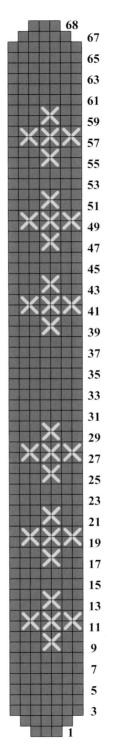

Choker Chart

Stitch Key for Choker

Wild Bill Hickock (MC)

Hopalong Cassidy (CC)

Cuff Chart

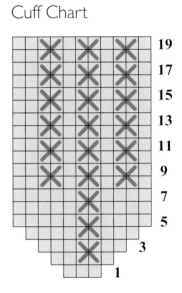

Stitch Key for Cuff
Hopalong Cassidy (MC)

Wild Bill Hickock (CC)

Cuff

With MC, ch 7. Join ch with a sl st forming a ring (button loop). Turn.

Row 1 Ch 1, work 3 sc in ring. Turn.

Row 2 Ch 1, work 2 sc in first st, sc in next st, work 2 sc in last st—5 sts. Turn.

Row 3 Ch 1, sc in each st across. Turn.

Row 4 Ch 1, work 2 sc in first st, sc in each st to last st, work 2 sc in last st—7 sts. Turn.

Rows 5–8 Rep rows 3 and 4 twice more—11 sts. Turn. Rep row 3 until piece measures 9"/23cm from row 1. To test-fit, wrap cuff around wrist so tip of button loop overlaps opposite end by approx 2¼"/5.5cm. Add or pull out as many rows as needed. When satisfied with length, join CC, ch 1, turn.

Edging

Rnd 1 (RS) Sc in each st across, working 2 sc in last st. Turn to side edge. Ch 1, sc in side edge of next row, *ch 1, sk next 2 rows, sc in side edge of next row; rep from * to side edge of row 1. Work 9 sc in bottom loop. Turn to opposite side edge. Sc in side edge of row 1. Rep from * to *, working sc in side edge of last row. Join rnd with a sl st in first st. Fasten off.

Finishing

Weave in ends.

Embroidery

Work chart using one strand of CC. Work each cross stitch over 2 sts and 2 rows making sure that yarn lies flat. With RS facing, beg chart on rows 2/3, working first cross stitch over sts 2 and 3. (**Note** The ch-1 t-ch at beg of each RS row counts as one st, but is not represented on the chart.) Work chart to row 19, then cont to rep rows 18 and 19 to the end. Sew on button to correspond to button loop. Position bottom half of snap on same side of cuff as button, placing it in center and ¼"/.6cm from short edge; sew in place. Sew on top half of snap to correspond to bottom half.)

timeless tassels

Slip-stitch crochet cords of metallic yarn are tied together to form a chunky tassel. Dotted throughout are sterling silver beads that add a touch of glint and glimmer. A great go-with is a tubular crocheted spiral of seed beads. Silver-plated metal tassels finish the ends beautifully.

Beaded Tassel Necklace

Finished Measurements
- Length after tying approx 18½"/47cm (including tassel)
- Width of strap approx 1"/2.5cm

Materials
- 1 .880oz/25g hank (approx 85yd/78m) of Berroco, Inc. *Metallic FX* (rayon/metallic (**3**)) in #1002 silver
- Size H/8 (5mm) crochet hook *or size to obtain gauge*
- Size 2 (2.25mm) steel crochet hook
- Thirty-two 8mm round large hole (3mm) sterling silver beads
- Eight 9mm round large hole (3mm) sterling silver beads
- Safety pin
- Bond 527 multipurpose cement or other clear, permanent adhesive
- Wire cutters
- Two bamboo skewers
- Paper plate

Gauge
20 sts to 4"/10cm over sl st using size H/8 (5mm) crochet hook.

Take time to check your gauge.

Necklace Strands (make 4)
With larger hook, ch 241.

Row 1 Sl st in 2nd ch from hook and in each ch across—240 sts. Fasten off. (**Note** Due to the slick texture of this yarn, you may find that not all strands will be the same length. This is expected and acceptable.)

Finishing
Weave in end.

Assembling necklace
Locate center of each strand, then use the safety pin to fasten all strands together at center points. Thread three 8mm beads on each strand end. To thread a bead, insert steel crochet hook through hole in bead. Catch the end of the strand with the hook, then draw the end through the bead hole. Slide the beads toward the center. Gather the strands together and make a neat overhand knot, approx 11½"/29cm from center point. You'll now have a tassel below the knot that measures approx 5½"/14cm long. Arrange beads along strands above the knot; as shown.

Onto each tassel strand, thread one 8mm bead and one 9mm bead. Slide 8mm beads towards knot. Slide 9mm bead about 1"/2.5cm from end of strand. Use wire cutters to cut each bamboo skewer in half. Reserve the pointed-end half and discard the other half. Snip off the tips to blunt them. Slide 9mm bead toward strand end, so bottom of bead is even with bottom of end. Using blunted tip of skewer, gently tuck the strand end inside the bead. Apply a small puddle of cement to the paper plate. Using the rem skewer, carefully apply cement inside the bead. Cont to work in this manner until all 9mm beads have been glued, taking care not to disturb those that are completed. Let dry 6 hours before moving. Slide 8mm beads to tops of 9mm beads.

Spiral Bracelet

Finished Measurements
- Length approx 20½"/52cm (uncoiled and excluding tassels; will adjust to most wrist sizes)
- Width of one coil approx ½"/1.5cm

Materials
- 1 ball (approx 131yd/120m) of DMC Inc. Size 12 *Pearl Cotton* (cotton) in #415 pearl gray
- Size 2 (2.25mm) steel crochet hook *or size to obtain gauge*
- Two hundred ninety-six size 6/0 "E" seed beads each in gunmetal (A) and matte gray (B)
- One hundred forty-eight size 6/0 "E" seed beads each in clear crystal silver-lined (C) and gray crystal silver-lined (D)
- Two 3mm round silver-plated beads
- Two 12mm antique silver cast-pewter bead caps
- Two 2½"/6.5cm-long silver-plated chain tassels with cone tops
- Seven continuous coils of bracelet memory wire
- Two chain-nose pliers

Stitch Glossary
SLB Slide bead next to crochet hook.

sc2tog [Insert hook in next st, yo and draw up a lp] twice, yo and draw through all 3 lps on hook.

- Round-nose pliers
- Memory-wire shears or heavy-duty wire cutters
- Any color sewing thread
- Size 7 or 8 sharps sewing needle

Gauge
6 sts to ⁷⁄₁₆"/1cm diameter and 28 rnds to 4"/10cm over tubular crochet using size 2 (2.25mm) steel crochet hook.
Take time to check your gauge.

Bracelet

Stringing beads
Using needle and thread technique, string seed beads onto perle cotton as foll: *A, B, C, A, B, D; rep from * until all beads are strung.

Tubular crochet
Ch 3. Join ch with a sl st forming a ring.

Rnd 1 Work 6 sc in ring. Do not join. You will be working in a spiral where rnds are not joined.

Rnd 2 [Insert hook in next st, SLB, yo and draw up a lp, yo and draw through both lps on hook] 6 times. You will now be working from the WS.

Rnd 3 [Insert hook under horizontal thread coming out of RH side of next bead of rnd below, SLB, yo and draw up a lp, yo and draw through both lps on hook] 6 times. Rep rnd 3 for tubular crochet and work until all beads are used.

Next rnd [Insert hook under horizontal thread coming out of RH side of next bead of rnd below, yo and draw up a lp, yo and draw through both lps on hook] 6 times.

Last rnd [Sc2tog] 3 times. Fasten off.

Finishing
Weave in ends.

Assembling bracelet
Use your hands to straighten out first three coils of memory wire. At opposite end of wire, use round-nose pliers to form a loop. Thread a 3mm bead and a bead cap onto wire and slide them to loop end. Insert straight end of memory wire through center of crocheted tube, taking care not to catch sts or beads. Slide crocheted tube along wire so end butts bead cap. Thread rem bead cap and 3mm bead onto wire and slide them along wire so bead cap butts end of crocheted tube. Use memory-wire shears to trim wire to ¼"/.6cm from 3mm bead. Use round-nose pliers to form end into loop. Connect tassel loops to memory-wire loops.

the allure of jade

Create a dramatic fashion accent with an intriguing faux-jade pendant attached to lacy crocheted ties. Add to it a multi-strand wrap bracelet that can do double duty as a pretty rope necklace.

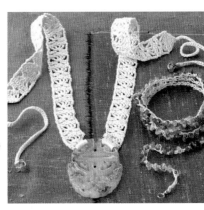

Faux-Jade Pendant Necklace

Finished Measurements
- Length approx 22"/56cm (excluding ties)
- Width of strap approx ¾"/2cm

Materials
- 1 ball (approx 350yd/311m) of South Maid/Coats & Clark *Size 10 Crochet Cotton* (mercerized cotton) in #429 new ecru
- Size 2 (2.25mm) steel crochet hook *or size to obtain gauge*
- One 2¼" x 1¾"/57 x 44mm oval synthetic jade Chinese pendant
- Six acrylic jade chips
- Any color sewing thread
- Size 7 or 8 sharps sewing needle
- Small safety pin

Stitch Glossary

sc2tog [Insert hook in next st, yo and draw up a lp] twice, yo and draw through all 3 lps on hook.

sc3tog [Insert hook in next st, yo and draw up a lp] 3 times, yo and draw through all 4 lps on hook.

Gauge
9 sts to ¾"/2cm and 20 rows to 3"/7.5cm over pat st using size 2 (2.25mm) steel crochet hook.
Take time to check your gauge.

Necklace
Right strap
Make a slip knot and place on hook. With WS of pendant facing, work 9 sc over right upper bar. Turn.

Row 1 (RS) Ch 1, sc in first st, ch 2, sk next 2 sts, sc in next 3 sts, ch 2, sk next 2 sts, sc in last st. Turn.

Row 2 Ch 1, sc in first st, work 2 sc over ch-2 sp, sc in next st, ch 3, sk next st, sc in next st, work 2 sc in ch-2 sp, sc in last st. Turn.

Row 3 Ch 5 (counts as 1 dtr), sk first 4 sts, in ch-3 sp work [tr, ch 1] 3 times, tr in same ch-3 sp, sk next 3 sts, dtr in last st. Turn.

Row 4 Ch 1, sc in first 2 sts, [sc in next ch-1 sp, sc in next st] 3 times, sc in sp between last st made and ch-5 t-ch. Turn. Rep rows 1–4 17 times more. Strap should measure approx 10¾"/27.5cm from beg. Turn.

Next row Ch 1, sc2tog, sc to last 2 sts, sc2tog—7 sts. Turn. Rep last row twice more—3 sts. Turn.

Next row Ch 1, sc3tog—1 st. Turn.

Tie
Ch 70. Remove lp from hook and fasten with safety pin. Cut crochet thread leaving a 2yd/2m tail. Using needle and thread technique, string three chips onto tail. Remove safety pin and place lp back on hook.

Next row Turn to bottom lps of ch, slide all three chips next to crochet hook, using thread coming from opposite side of last chip hole, sl st in first bottom lp, then sl in each of next 69 bottom lps. Fasten off.

Left strap

Make a slip knot and place on hook. With WS of pendant facing, work 9 sc over left upper bar. Cont to work as for right strap.

Finishing

Weave in ends.

Wrap Bracelet/Rope Necklace

Finished Measurements

Five-strand wrap bracelet

- Circumference approx 8"/20.5cm (including clasp)

Rope necklace

- Length approx 39½"/100.5cm (including clasp)

Materials

- 1 ball (approx 350yd/311m) of South Maid/Coats & Clark *Size 10 Crochet Cotton* (mercerized cotton) in #429 new ecru
- Size 2 (2.25mm) steel crochet hook
- One hundred forty-five acrylic jade chips
- One 14.5 x 7.5mm silver-plated lobster-claw clasp
- One 6mm round silver-plated jump ring
- Two 3mm round silver-plated beads
- Two silver crimp beads
- Crimping pliers (optional)
- Any color sewing thread
- Size 7 or 8 sharps sewing needle

Stitch Glossary

SLC Slide chip next to crochet hook. Make next ch using thread coming from opposite side of chip hole.

Gauge

Gauge is not important.

Bracelet/Necklace

Thread chips onto crochet thread using the needle and thread technique. Make a slip knot leaving a long tail. Place slip knot on hook.

Row 1 Ch 8, *SLC, ch 2; rep from *, end ch 6.
Fasten off leaving a long tail.

Finishing

Using needle and thread technique, string a 3mm bead, crimp bead and clasp loop onto one tail. Skipping the clasp loop, insert needle back through crimp bead and 3mm bead. Remove needle and thread. Pull on tail to remove slack. Use crimping pliers to crimp bead. Weave in tail. Rep at opposite end, stringing on a 3mm bead, crimp bead and jump ring. To wear as a bracelet, wrap five times around wrist, then fasten closed.

bonus earrings (make 2)

For each earring, connect a silver Chinese "good luck" character charm to a 1½"/4cm silver-plated eyepin. Onto same eyepin, thread a 3mm silver-plated bead, five acrylic jade chips and another 3mm silver-plated bead. Make a loop at end of eyepin, connecting it to a silver fishhook earwire.

passion for pearls

Tiny gold beads crocheted with black cotton thread contrast dramatically with oversized white pearls. This stunning rope necklace partners perfectly with gold beaded earrings.

Pearl and Bead Necklace

Finished Measurements

- Length before final assembly approx 42"/106.5cm
- Width approx ⅝"/1.6m

Materials

- 1 ball (approx 284yd/260m) of DMC Inc. *Cebelia Size 10 Crochet Cotton* (mercerized cotton) in #310 black
- Size 2 (2.25mm) steel crochet hook *or size to obtain gauge*
- Five hundred twenty 4mm round gold-plated beads
- Ten 16mm round white pearls
- Forty 4mm round gold-plated disc beads
- Twenty 8mm gold-plated cord caps
- Thirty 1½"/4cm gold-plated eyepins
- Chain-nose pliers
- Round-nose pliers
- Wire cutters

Stitch Glossary

SLB Slide bead next to crochet hook.

sc2tog [Insert hook in next st, yo and draw up a lp] twice, yo and draw through all 3 lps on hook.

- Any color sewing thread
- Size 7 or 8 sharps sewing needle

Gauge

4 sts to ⁷⁄₁₆"/1cm diameter and 13 rnds to 2¼"/5.5cm over tubular crochet using size 2 (2.25mm) steel crochet hook.

Take time to check your gauge.

Necklace Segments (make 10)

Stringing beads

Using needle and thread technique, string fifty-two 4mm beads onto crochet thread.

Tubular crochet

Ch 3. Join ch with a sl st forming a ring.

Rnd 1 Work 4 sc in ring. Do not join. You will be working in a spiral where rnds are not joined.

Rnd 2 [Insert hook in next st, SLB, yo and draw up a lp, yo and draw through both lps on hook] 4 times. You will now be working from the WS.

Rnd 3 [Insert hook under horizontal thread coming out of RH side of next bead of rnd below, SLB, yo and draw up a lp, yo and draw through both lps on hook] 4 times. Rep rnd 3 for tubular crochet and work until all beads are used.

Next rnd [Insert hook under horizontal thread coming out of RH side of next bead of rnd below, yo and draw up a lp, yo and draw through both lps on hook] 4 times.

Last rnd [Sc2tog] twice. Fasten off.

Finishing

Weave in ends.

Attaching cord caps

Open loop end of an eyepin. Insert shaft of eyepin through center of one end of necklace segment. Draw eyepin through, hooking the crocheted fabric with the open loop. Close the loop, securing the eyepin to the fabric. Thread on a cord cap, then a disc bead. Form end of eyepin into a loop. Rep at opposite end of necklace segment. Cont to work in this manner until all necklace segments have cord caps.

Assembling necklace

Connect an eyepin to a necklace segment loop. Onto same eyepin, thread a disc bead, pearl and another disc bead. Form end of eyepin into a loop, connecting it to another necklace segment loop. Cont to work in this manner until all necklace segments are connected to pearls.

Beaded Loop Earrings

Finished Measurement
- Length approx 2¾"/7cm

Materials
- I ball (approx 284yd/260m) of DMC Inc. *Cebelia Size 10 Crochet Cotton* (mercerized cotton) in #310 black
- Size 2 (2.25mm) steel crochet hook *or size to obtain gauge*
- One pair 11mm round gold-plated post earrings with drops
- Two hundred twenty 3mm round gold-plated beads
- Four 8mm gold-plated cord caps
- Four 1½"/4cm gold-plated eyepins
- Two 6mm round gold-plated jump rings
- Two 5mm round gold-plated jump rings
- Two chain-nose pliers
- Round-nose pliers

Stitch Glossary
SLB Slide bead next to crochet hook.

sc2tog [Insert hook in next st, yo and draw up a lp] twice, yo and draw through all 3 lps on hook.

- Wire cutters
- Any color sewing thread
- Size 7 or 8 sharps sewing needle

Gauge
4 sts to ⅜"/1cm diameter and 27 rnds to 4½"/11.5cm over tubular crochet using size 2 (2.25mm) steel crochet hook.

Take time to check your gauge.

Earrings (make 2)
Stringing beads
Set aside two 3mm beads for finishing. Using needle and thread technique, string one hundred eight 3mm beads onto crochet thread.

Tubular crochet
Ch 2. Join ch with a sl st forming a ring.

Rnd 1 Work 4 sc in ring. Do not join. You will be working in a spiral where rnds are not joined.

Rnd 2 [Insert hook in next st, SLB, yo and draw up a lp, yo and draw through both lps on hook] 4 times. You will now be working from the WS.

Rnd 3 [Insert hook under horizontal thread coming out of RH side of next bead of rnd below, SLB, yo and draw up a lp, yo and draw through both lps on hook] 4 times. Rep rnd 3 for tubular crochet and work until all beads are used.

Next rnd [Insert hook under horizontal thread coming out of RH side of next bead of rnd below, yo and draw up a lp, yo and draw through both lps on hook] 4 times.

Last rnd [Sc2tog] twice. Fasten off.

Finishing
Weave in ends.
Attaching cord caps
Open loop end of an eyepin. Insert shaft of eyepin through center of one end of crocheted tube segment. Draw eyepin through, hooking the crocheted fabric with the open loop. Close the loop, securing the eyepin to the fabric. Thread on a cord cap, then a 3mm bead. Form end of eyepin into a loop. Rep at opposite end of crocheted tube. Attach rem cord caps to rem crocheted tube.

Assembling earrings
For each earring, connect crocheted tube loops to a 6mm jump ring. Join 6mm jump ring to earstud drop with a 5mm jump ring.

tied and true

A single strand of cluster stitches speckled with gold corrugated beads makes a dainty tied necklace. Drop-hoop earrings feature flirty chain fringes. You can use longer fringes for a more flamboyant look or eliminate them for a simpler style.

Tasseled Lariat

Finished Measurements
- Length approx 31"/79cm (excluding tassels)
- Width approx ⅜"/1cm

Materials
- 1 ball (approx 284yd/260m) of DMC Inc. *Cebelia Size 10 Crochet Cotton* (mercerized cotton) in #816 garnet
- Size 2 (2.25mm) steel crochet hook *or size to obtain gauge*
- Sixty-six 4mm round gold-plated corrugated beads
- Two 2½"/6.5cm-long gold-plated chain tassels with cone tops
- Any color sewing thread
- Size 7 or 8 sharps sewing needle

Stitch Glossary
TRCL (treble crochet cluster) In same sc (or ch) work [yo twice, insert hook in sc (or ch), yo and draw up a lp, (yo and draw through 2 lps on hook) twice] 4 times, yo and draw through all 5 lps on hook.

SLB Slide bead next to crochet hook.

Gauge
1 TRCL to ⅜"/1cm and 22 rows to 5"/12.5cm over bead pat st using size 2 (2.25mm) steel crochet hook.

Take time to check your gauge.

Necklace

Stringing beads
Using needle and thread technique, string all beads onto crochet thread.

Beg bead pat st
Ch 5, leaving a long tail for sewing.

Row 1 (RS) Work TRCL in 5th ch from hook. Ch 1, turn.

Row 2 SLB, sc in top of TRCL. Ch 4, turn.

Row 3 Work TRCL in sc. Ch 1, turn. Rep rows 2 and 3 for pat st and work until all beads have been used, end with row 3; do not ch and turn. Fasten off leaving a long tail for sewing.

Finishing
At one end of necklace, thread tail into sewing needle. Use tail to sew tassel to necklace. Weave in thread securely and invisibly. Repeat for the other end.

The lariat-style necklace can be worn several different ways (see page 55 for ideas).

Drop-Hoop Earrings

Finished Measurement
- Length approx 2½"/6.5cm

Materials
- 1 ball (approx 284yd/260m) of DMC Inc. *Cebelia Size 10 Crochet Cotton* (mercerized cotton) in #816 garnet
- Size 2 (2.25mm) steel crochet hook
- One pair 8mm half-ball gold-plated earstuds with drops
- Two gold-plated barrel earnuts
- Two 1⅛"/28.5mm cabone rings (also called bone rings)
- Four 8mm round gold-plated jump rings
- One 11"/28cm length of 3.1mm gold-plated curb chain
- Two chain-nose pliers
- Wire cutters
- Size 26 chenille needle

Gauge
Gauge is not important.

✣ **Note** You will find it helpful to use pliers to pull the chenille needle through when weaving in ends.

Earrings (make 2)
Covering ring
Make a slip knot, leaving a 6"/15cm tail, and place on hook.

Rnd 1 (RS) Working fairly tightly, sc over cabone ring until ring is completely covered. Do not join. Cut thread leaving a 6"/15cm tail. Do not fasten off, just draw this end tail through last st. Thread end tail in chenille needle. Insert needle into top of first sc, draw thread through. On WS, weave in end tail, then weave in beg tail.

Finishing
Making chain fringe
For each fringe, cut three 15-link (approx 1⅝"/4cm) lengths of chain.

Assembling earrings
For each earring, open a jump ring and thread on covered ring. Connect jump ring to the earring drop making sure that RS of covered ring faces out. Thread three lengths of chain onto another jump ring. Connect this jump ring to previous jump ring. Position fringe in front of covered ring or behind.

simply charming

Silky crocheted beads blend beautifully with shiny gold charms to make a fun bracelet, necklace and earrings ensemble.

Charm-Holder Necklace

Finished Measurements
- Length approx 25"/63.5cm (excluding bead and charms)
- Bead approx 2"/51mm long (including top and bottom loops)

Materials
- 1 spool (approx 101yd/93m) of Gudebrod *Champion Silk Thread Size FFF* in royal blue
- Size 2 (2.25mm) steel crochet hook
- One 20 x 14mm oval wooden bead in dark brown
- Two 3mm round gold-plated corrugated beads
- One 25"/63.5 length of 7mm gold-plated fancy file cable chain
- One 7"/17.5cm length of 3.1mm gold-plated curb chain
- Five gold-plated stamped brass charms (Victorian charm mix and Heart charm mix shown here)
- Two 14mm antique gold cast-pewter end caps
- One 1½"/4cm gold-plated eyepin

Stitch Glossary

sc2tog [Insert hook in next st, yo and draw up a lp] twice, yo and draw through all 3 lps on hook.

- One 8mm round gold-plated split ring
- Ten 5mm round gold-plated jump rings
- One 12mm round gold-plated jump ring
- One 8 x 5mm oval gold-plated jump ring
- Small safety pin
- Two chain-nose pliers
- Round-nose pliers
- Wire cutters

Gauge
Gauge is not important.

Necklace
Covering bead
Ch 3. Join ch with a sl st forming a ring.

Rnd 1 (RS) Ch 1, work 5 sc in ring. Mark last st made with the safety pin. You will be working in a spiral marking the last st made with the safety pin to indicate end of rnd.

Rnd 2 [Work 2 sc in next st] 5 times—10 sts.

Rnd 3 [Work 2 sc in next st] 10 times—20 sts.

Rnds 4–12 Sc in each st around. When rnd 12 is completed, insert wooden bead into covering, matching up hole in bead with center hole of rnd 1. To align the two holes, insert the crochet hook into the wooden bead, then into the covering so it exits the hole. Bring covering up sides of bead; remove safety pin. Working into sts with covering on bead, cont to work as foll:

Rnd 13 [Sc2tog] 10 times—10 sts.

Rnd 14 [Sc2tog] 5 times—5 sts.

Rnd 15 Sc in first st, [sc2tog] twice—3 sts. Fasten off.

Finishing
Weave in ends.

Assembling bead
Onto the eyepin, thread a corrugated bead, a cone, crocheted bead, another cone and another corrugated bead. Form end of eyepin into a loop.

Assembling necklace
Connect the two ends of the fancy file cable chain together with the split ring, making sure the chain is not twisted. Connect the assembled bead to center of fancy file cable chain with the oval jump ring. Connect 12mm jump ring to eyepin loop of assembled

bead. Determine desired lengths of curb chain on which to hang five charms. The longest chain shown is 2½"/6.5cm (including jump rings and charm), and the shortest is 1½"/4cm (including jump rings and charm). Cut chain to determined lengths. Connect charms to chains using 5mm jump rings. Use 5mm jump rings to connect opposite ends of chains to 12mm ring, making sure all charms face out.

Charm Bracelet

Finished Measurements
- Length aprox 7½"/19cm
- Bead approx 1¾"/44mm long (including top loop)

Materials
- 1 spool (approx 101yd/93m) of Gudebrod *Champion Silk Thread Size FFF* in royal blue
- Size 2 (2.25mm) steel crochet hook
- Six 18 x 10mm oval wooden beads in dark brown
- Twelve 3mm round gold-plated corrugated beads
- One 7½"/19cm long 4.6mm gold-plated curb chain charm bracelet
- Thirteen to fourteen gold-plated stamped brass charms (Victorian charm mix and Heart charm mix shown here)
- Twelve 10 x 7mm antique gold cast-pewter floral cones
- Twelve 1½"/4cm gold-plated headpins
- Nineteen to twenty 6mm round gold-plated jump rings
- Small safety pin
- Two chain-nose pliers
- Round-nose pliers
- Wire cutters

Stitch Glossary

sc2tog [Insert hook in next st, yo and draw up a lp] twice, yo and draw through all 3 lps on hook.

Gauge
Gauge is not important.

Bracelet
Covering beads (make 6)
Ch 3. Join ch with a sl st forming a ring.

Rnd 1 (RS) Ch 1, work 6 sc in ring. Mark last st made with the safety pin. You will be working in a spiral marking the last st made with the safety pin to indicate end of rnd.

Rnd 2 [Sc in next st, work 2 sc in next st] 3 times—9 sts.

Rnd 3 [Sc in next 2 sts, work 2 sc in next st] 3 times—12 sts.

Rnd 4 [Sc in next 3 sts, work 2 sc in next st] 3 times—15 sts.

Rnds 5–10 Sc in each st around. When rnd 10 is completed, insert wooden bead into covering, matching up hole in bead with center hole of rnd 1. To align the two holes, insert the crochet hook into the wooden bead, then into the covering so it exits the hole. Bring covering up sides of bead; remove safety pin. Working into sts with covering on bead, cont to work as foll:

Rnd 11 [Sc in next 3 sts, sc2tog] 3 times—12 sts.

Rnd 12 [Sc2tog] 6 times—6 sts.

Rnd 13 [Sc2tog] 3 times—3 sts. Fasten off.

Finishing
Weave in ends.
Assembling beads
Thread a corrugated bead onto a headpin. Onto same headpin, thread a cone, crocheted bead, another cone and a corrugated bead. Form end of headpin into a loop.
Assembling bracelet
Plan spacing of crocheted beads and charms along bracelet. Using jump rings to connect beads and charms to bracelet, connect crocheted beads first, then charms.

Oval Bead Earrings

Finished Measurement
- Length approx 2⅛"/5.5cm

Materials
- 1 spool (approx 101yd/93m) of Gudebrod *Champion Silk Thread Size FFF* in royal blue
- Size 2 (2.25mm) steel crochet hook
- Two 18 x 10mm oval wooden beads in dark brown
- Four 3mm round gold-plated corrugated beads
- One pair 15mm round gold-filled hoop earrings
- Two 10 x 7mm antique gold cast-pewter floral cones
- Two 1½"/4cm gold-plated headpins
- Two 6mm round gold-plated jump rings
- Small safety pin
- Two chain-nose pliers
- Round-nose pliers
- Wire cutters

Stitch Glossary
sc2tog [Insert hook in next st, yo and draw up a lp] twice, yo and draw through all 3 lps on hook.

Gauge
Gauge is not important.

Earrings (make 2)
Covering bead
Ch 3. Join ch with a sl st forming a ring.

Rnd 1 (RS) Ch 1, work 6 sc in ring. Mark last st made with the safety pin. You will be working in a spiral marking the last st made with the safety pin to indicate end of rnd.

Rnd 2 [Sc in next st, work 2 sc in next st] 3 times—9 sts.

Rnd 3 [Sc in next 2 sts, work 2 sc in next st] 3 times—12 sts.

Rnd 4 [Sc in next 3 sts, work 2 sc in next st] 3 times—15 sts.

Rnds 5–10 Sc in each st around. When rnd 10 is completed, insert wooden bead into covering, matching up hole in bead with center hole of rnd 1. To align the two holes, insert the crochet hook into the wooden bead, then into the covering so it exits the hole. Bring covering up sides of bead; remove safety pin. Working into sts with covering on bead, cont to work as foll:

Rnd 11 [Sc in next 3 sts, sc2tog] 3 times—12 sts.

Rnd 12 [Sc2tog] 6 times—6 sts.

Rnd 13 [Sc2tog] 3 times—3 sts. Fasten off.

Finishing
Weave in ends.

Assembling earrings
For each earring, thread a corrugated bead onto a headpin. Onto same headpin, thread a crocheted bead, a cone and another corrugated bead. Form end of headpin into a loop. Connect a jump ring to loop. Thread hoop through jump ring.

Crocheted beads add an instant touch of color to any hoop earrings. Make them in colors to match your wardrobe.

deco dazzle

This elegant collar necklace adorned with hematite and silver beads is assembled using chrome-plated metal links. Simple rectangular earrings complete the look.

Beaded Collar Necklace

Finished Measurements
- Inner circumference (fastened in first link of chain) approx 16½"/42cm (adjustable to approx 19¼"/49cm)
- Width approx 1"/2.5cm

Materials
- 1 ball (approx 284yd/260m) of DMC Inc. *Cebelia Size 10 Crochet Cotton* (mercerized cotton) in #3033 mocha brown
- Size 2 (2.25mm) steel crochet hook *or size to obtain gauge*
- Four 16"/40.5cm strands (approx one hundred nine beads per strand) of 4mm round glass hematite beads
- Ninety-six 4mm round sterling silver seamless-look beads
- Seven 1"/25mm nickel-plated rectangle rings by Dritz
- One set antique silver cast-pewter five-hole end bar with chain and lobster-claw clasp
- Size 26 chenille needle
- Matching sewing thread
- Size 7 or 8 sharps sewing needle

Gauge
12 sts and 12 rows to 1"/2.5cm over bead pat st using size 2 (2.25mm) steel crochet hook.
Take time to check your gauge.

Stitch Glossary
SLH Slide hematite bead next to crochet hook.
SLS Slide silver bead next to crochet hook.

Necklace Sections (make 8)

Stringing beads
Using needle and thread technique, string beads onto crochet thread as foll: [12 hematite, 4 silver] 3 times, end 12 hematite.

Beg bead pat st
Ch 13, leaving a long tail for sewing.

Row 1 Sc in 2nd ch from hook and in each ch across—12 sts. Turn.

Rows 2–8 Ch 1, sc in each st across. Turn.

Row 9 (WS) Ch 1, sc in first st, [SLH, sc in next st, sc in following st] 5 times, SLH, sc in last st. Turn.

Row 10 Rep row 2.

Row 11 Rep row 9.

Row 12 (short row) Ch 1, sc in first 8 sts. Turn.

Row 13 (short row) Ch 1, sc in first st, [SLS, sc in next st, sc in following st] 3 times, SLS, sc in last st. Turn.

Row 14 Ch 1, sc in first 8 sts, then sc in next 4 sts of 2 rows below. Turn.

Rows 15–26 Rep rows 9–14 twice more.

Rows 27–29 Rep rows 9–11 once more.

Rows 30–36 Rep row 2. Fasten off leaving a long tail for sewing.

Finishing
Fold right end of a section in half over a rectangle ring. Thread tail into a chenille needle and hem. Cont as foll: *Fold left end of next section in half over opposite side of last rectangle ring; hem. Fold right end of section in half over next rectangle ring; hem; rep from * until all eight sections have been joined to rectangle rings. Fold

two rem ends ⅜"/1cm over to WS and hem. Position lobster-claw end bar on RS of right end of necklace. Have top edge of end bar even with top edge of necklace. Sew in place using sewing needle and thread. Rep for chain end bar and left end of necklace.

Rectangular Earrings

Finished Measurement
- Length approx 2"/5cm

Materials
- 1 ball (approx 284yd/260m) of DMC Inc. *Cebelia Size 10 Crochet Cotton* (mercerized cotton) in #3033 mocha brown
- Size 2 (2.25mm) steel crochet hook
- Two 1"/25mm nickel-plated rectangle rings by Dritz
- One pair 17 x 17mm three-quarter square silver-plated earrings with drops
- Two silver-plated barrel earnuts
- Two 9 x 5mm silver-plated smooth-finish ribbon end crimps
- Two chain-nose pliers
- Size 26 chenille needle

Gauge
Gauge is not important.

❊ **Note** You will find it helpful to use pliers to pull the chenille needle through when weaving in ends.

Earrings (make 2)
Covering rectangle ring
Rnd 1 (RS) Make a slip knot leaving a 4"/10cm tail, then place on hook. Join thread to the rectangle ring with a sc. Making sure to work tightly and evenly, work approx 20 sc over ring, then slide the sts so first st made is now in center of one short end of ring (this is now the center top). Cont to sc over ring until it is completely covered. Cut thread leaving a 6"/15cm tail. Do not fasten off, just draw this end tail through last st. Thread end tail in chenille needle. Insert needle into top of first sc, draw yarn through. On WS, weave in end tail, then weave in beg tail.

Finishing
Attaching end crimps
With WS of covered ring and teeth side of end crimp facing, insert the center top edge into the crimp. Position the crimp so it is parallel with the edge of the ring and the teeth of the crimp are embedded in the crocheted fabric. Squeeze the crimp closed using pliers. Squeeze at right-side edge of crimp, then at left-side edge to ensure an even closure.
Assembling earrings
For each earring, connect the end crimp loop to the earring drop making sure that RS of covered ring faces out.

silk and satin

Create an elegant sash-tie necklace with pure silk thread and satin-finish beads. Match it with a coordinating cuff bracelet that fastens with a pretty toggle clasp, and round out the ensemble with crocheted bead dangle earrings.

Sash-Tie Necklace

Finished Measurements
- Length approx 38"/96.5cm
- Width approx 1¼"/3cm

Materials
- 1 spool (approx 101yd/93m) of Gudebrod *Champion Silk Thread Size FFF* in navy blue
- Size 2 (2.25mm) steel crochet hook *or size to obtain gauge*
- Four 16"/40.5cm strands (approx one hundred ten beads per strand) of 4mm round satin-finish druk beads in dark blue
- Any color sewing thread
- Size 7 or 8 sharps sewing needle

Stitch Glossary

SLB Slide bead next to crochet hook.

MBP (make beaded picot) Work (sc, SLB, ch 1, sc) in same ch.

Gauge
16 sts to 1¼"/3cm and 17 rows to 4"/10cm over beaded pat st using size 2 (2.25mm) steel crochet hook.

Take time to check your gauge.

Necklace
Right half
Stringing beads

Using needle and thread technique, string two hundred beads onto silk thread.

Beg bead pat st

Ch 17.

Foundation row (RS) Sc in 2nd ch from hook, *ch 7, sk next 4 ch, sc in next ch; rep from * to end—3 ch-7 lps. Turn.

Row 1 (WS) *Ch 7, MBP in 4th ch of next ch-7 lp; rep from *, end ch 3, tr in last sc. Turn.

Row 2 Ch 1, sc in tr, *ch 7, MBP in 4th ch of next ch-7 lp; rep from *, end ch 7, sc in 4th ch of last ch-7 lp. Turn.
Rep rows 1 and 2 39 times more. Turn.

Next row *Ch 7, sc in 4th ch of next ch-7 lp; rep from *, end ch 3, tr in last sc. Turn.

Last row Ch 1, sc in tr, work 3 sc over ch-3, [work 7 sc over next ch-7 lp] twice, work 3 sc over last ch-7 lp, then sc in 4th ch of same lp. Fasten off.

Left half
Stringing beads

Using needle and thread technique, string two hundred beads onto silk thread.

Beg bead pat st

Position right half so RS is facing and bottom lps of foundation ch are at top.

Foundation row (RS) Make a slip knot and place on hook, insert hook into first bottom lp, yo and draw up a lp, yo and draw

through both lps on hook, *ch 7, sk next 4 bottom lps, sc in next bottom lp; rep from * to end—3 ch-7 lps. Turn. Beg with row 1, cont to work as for right half.

Finishing

Weave in ends. Working on a thick terry towel, press necklace using a dampened pressing cloth.

Pavé Bead Bracelet

Finished Measurements

- Length approx 7⅞"/20cm (including toggle clasp)
- Width approx 1¼"/3cm

Materials

- 2 cards (each approx 14yd/13m) of Gudebrod *Champion Silk Thread* Size FFF in navy blue
- Size 2 (2.25mm) steel crochet hook *or size to obtain gauge*
- Two 16"/40.5cm strands (approx one hundred ten beads per strand) of 4mm round satin-finish druk beads in dark blue
- Two 19 x 5mm gold-plated smooth-finish ribbon end crimps
- Two 8 x 5mm oval gold-plated jump rings
- One 18 x 13mm antique gold cast-pewter banded bar-and-ring toggle clasp
- Two chain-nose pliers
- Size 26 chenille needle
- Any color sewing thread
- Size 7 or 8 sharps sewing needle

Stitch Glossary

SLB Slide bead next to crochet hook.

sc2tog [Insert hook in next st, yo and draw up a lp] twice, yo and draw through all 3 lps on hook.

Gauge

10 sts to 1"/2.5cm and 22 rows to 2"/5cm over beaded pat st using size 2 (2.25mm) steel crochet hook.

Take time to check your gauge.

✳ **Note** You will find it helpful to use pliers to pull the chenille needle through when weaving in ends.

Bracelet

Stringing beads

Using needle and thread technique, string one strand of beads onto each card of silk thread.

Beg bead pat st

With first card of silk thread, ch 7.

Row 1 (RS) Sc in 2nd ch from hook and in each ch across—6 sts. Ch 1, turn.

Row 2 Work 2 sc in first st, sc in next 4 sts, work 2 sc n last st—8 sts. SLB, ch 1, turn.

Row 3 Work 2 sc in first st, sc in next 6 sts, work 2 sc in last st—10 sts. SLB, ch 1, turn.

Row 4 Sc in first st, *SLB, sc in next 2 sts; rep from *, end SLB, sc in last st. SLB, ch 1, turn.

Row 5 Sc in each st across. SLB, ch 1, turn.

Row 6 Sc in first 2 sts, *SLB, sc in next 2 sts; rep from * to end. SLB, ch 1, turn.

Row 7 Rep row 5. Rep rows 4–7 15 times more (using second card of silk thread when necessary), then row 4 once.

Next row Sc2tog, sc in next 6 sts, sc2tog—8 sts. SLB, ch 1, turn.

Next row Sc2tog, sc in next 4 sts, sc2tog—6 sts. Ch 1, turn.

Last row Sc in each st across. Fasten off.

Finishing

Weave in ends using chenille needle. Working on a thick terry towel, press necklace using a dampened pressing cloth.

Attaching end crimps

With RS of bracelet facing, insert one end into the crimp. Position the crimp so it is centered side to side and the teeth of the crimp are embedded in the crocheted fabric. Squeeze the crimp closed using pliers. Squeeze at right-side edge of crimp, then at left-side edge to ensure an even closure. Rep at opposite end.

Attaching toggle clasp

Attach each portion of toggle clasp to end crimps with oval jump rings.

Crocheted Dangle Earrings

Finished Measurement

- Length approx 3¼"/8cm

Materials

- 1 card (approx 14yd/13m) of *Gudebrod Champion Silk Thread Size FFF* in navy blue
- Size 2 (2.25mm) steel crochet hook *or size to obtain gauge*
- Two 16mm round unfinished wooden balls with holes
- One pair antique gold post earrings with chandelier drops
- Four 4mm round satin-finish druk beads in dark blue
- Four 10mm antique gold round rimmed cast-pewter bead caps
- Two 16mm gold-plated column drops
- Two 1½"/4cm gold-plated eyepins
- Chain-nose pliers
- Round-nose pliers
- Wire cutters
- Small safety pin

Stitch Glossary

sc2tog [Insert hook in next st, yo and draw up a lp] twice, yo and draw through all 3 lps on hook.

Gauge

Work rnds 1–10 of bead covering using size 2 (2.25mm) steel crochet hook. Insert wooden bead into covering. The covering should fit snugly, but not so tightly that stitches are overstretched. The covering should also cover about two-thirds of the bead. Adjust steel crochet hook size if necessary.

Take time to check your gauge.

Earrings (make 2)

Bead covering

Ch 3. Join ch with a sl st forming a ring.

Rnd 1 (RS) Ch 1, work 6 sc in ring. Mark last st made with the safety pin. You will be working in a spiral marking the last st made with the safety pin to indicate end of rnd.

Rnd 2 [Work 2 sc in next st] 6 times—12 sts.

Rnd 3 [Sc in next st, work 2 sc in next st] 6 times—18 sts.

Rnds 4–10 Sc in each st around. When rnd 10 is completed, insert wooden bead into covering, matching up hole in bead with center hole of rnd 1. To align the two holes, insert the crochet hook into the wooden bead, then into the covering so it exits the hole. Bring covering up sides of bead; remove safety pin. Working into sts with covering on bead, cont to work as foll:

Rnd 11 [Sc in next st, sc2tog] 6 times—12 sts.

Rnd 12 [Sc2tog] 6 times—6 sts.

Rnd 13 [Sc2tog] 3 times—3 sts. Fasten off.

Finishing

Weave in ends.

Assembling earrings

For each earring, connect eyepin loop to column drop loop. Onto same eyepin, thread a 4mm bead, bead cap, crocheted bead, another bead cap and another 4mm bead. Form end of eyepin into a loop, connecting it to bottom center hole of chandelier drop.

colorful cloisonné

Brightly colored cloisonné beads pair perfectly with equally bright shades of silky yarn.
The single-tie rope necklace features graceful beaded drops at each end. Two of the bangles
also feature drops, while the third sports a fun fringe of beads around the perimeter.

Rope Necklace

Finished Measurements

- Length approx 36"/91.5cm
- Width approx ½"/1.5cm

Materials

- 1 1¾oz/50g hank (approx
85yd/70m) of Berroco, Inc.
Cotton Twist (mercerized cotton/
rayon 4) in #8364 icepop
- Size 7 (4.5mm) crochet hook
- Two 21 x 15mm flat oval
cloisonné beads in red
- Two 12 x 6mm teardrop
cloisonné beads in pink
- Two 3mm round gold-plated
beads
- Two 14mm gold-plated end
caps

- Four 1½"/4cm gold-plated
eyepins
- Two 1½"/4cm gold-plated
headpins
- Two chain-nose pliers
- Round-nose pliers
- Wire cutters

Gauge

Gauge is not important.

Necklace

Ch 3. Join ch with a sl st forming a ring.

Rnd 1 Ch 1, work 5 sc in ring. Do not join with a sl st. You will be
working in a continuous spiral where rnds are not joined.

Rnd 2 Working through back lps only, sc in next 5 sts. You will now
be working from the inside (WS) of the tube that is being formed.
Rep rnd 2 until piece measures approx 32"/81cm from beg. Fasten
off leaving an 8"/20.5cm end. Thread tail into tapestry needle and
weave through sts. Pull tight to gather, fasten off securely.

Finishing

Weave in ends.

Assembling necklace

For each end of necklace, open an eyepin loop. Insert opposite
end under the crocheted fabric at center end of necklace. Draw
eyepin through, catching the fabric in the opened loop. Close the
loop securing the fabric. Thread an end cap and a 3mm gold bead
onto this eyepin. Form end of eyepin into a loop. Thread an oval
bead onto another eyepin. Form end into a loop and connect it to
the end cap loop. Thread a teardrop bead onto a headpin. Form
end into a loop and connect it to the oval bead loop.

bonus earrings (make 2)

For each earring, thread a 12 x 6mm teardrop cloisonné bead
onto a 1½"/4cm gold-plated headpin. Make a loop at end
and connect it to a 1½"/4cm eyepin. Onto this eyepin, thread a
22 x 10mm heart cloisonné bead. Make a loop at end,
connecting it to another 1½"/4cm eyepin. Onto this eyepin,
thread a 6mm round cloisonné bead. Make a loop at end of
eyepin and connect it to a gold-filled fishhook earwire.

Trio of Bangles

Finished Measurement

- Inner circumference approx 8¼"/21cm
- Outer circumference approx 10"/25.5cm

Materials

- 1 1¾oz/50g hank (each approx 85yd/70m) each of Berroco, Inc. *Cotton Twist* (mercerized cotton/rayon (4)) in #8347 frankenberry, #8348 orange zinnia or #8311 true red
- Size G/6 (4mm) crochet hook
- One 3"/76mm diameter gold-tone welded metal ring

Frankenberry bracelet

- One 22 x 10mm heart cloisonné bead in pink
- Two 6mm round cloisonné beads in pink
- Any color sewing thread
- Size 7 or 8 sharps sewing needle

Orange zinnia bracelet

- Thirteen 10mm round cloisonné beads in green with attached loops (see note)
- Thirteen 7mm round gold-plated jump rings
- Two chain-nose pliers

True red bracelet

- Two 19 x 15mm butterfly cloisonné beads in blue
- Four 6mm round cloisonné beads in red
- Any color sewing thread
- Size 7 or 8 sharps sewing needle

Gauge

Gauge is not important.

✤ **Note** If cloisonné beads with attached loops are not available, you can get the same effect by threading each bead onto a headpin, then forming end of headpin into a loop. If you use this option, you will also need thirteen 1½"/4cm gold-plated headpins, chain-nose pliers, round-nose pliers and wire cutters.

Bangles

Covering metal ring

Make a slip knot leaving an 8"/20.5cm end. Place slip knot on hook.

Rnd 1 Working tightly, sc over ring until almost completely covered. Turn free end of work around the ring to form a ridged spiral. Cont to sc over ring and turn free end until there are twenty-five spiral ridges. For Frankenberry and True Red Bracelets, fasten off, leaving an 8"/20.5cm end. For Orange Zinnia Bracelet, cut yarn, leaving an 8"/20.5cm end; do not fasten off, just draw end through last st.

Finishing

Assembling frankenberry bracelet

Tie ends into a firm square knot. Using needle and thread technique for stringing beads, string a 6mm bead, heart bead and remaining 6mm bead onto both yarn ends held togther. Make an overhand knot close to last bead. Trim yarn ½"/1.3cm from bottom of last knot. Using the tip of the sewing needle, separate yarn strands to form a tassel.

Assembling orange zinnia bracelet

Thread end tail in tapesty needle. Insert needle into top of first sc, draw yarn through. On WS, weave in end tail, then weave in beg tail; this forms another ridge. Use pliers to open a jump ring. Skip the ridge formed by weaving in ends. On the next ridge, insert jump ring under outermost st. You might find it helpful to hold jump ring with one pair of pliers rather than using your fingers. Thread on bead, then close jump ring. Working in this manner, continue to connect a bead to outermost st of every other ridge around.

Assembling true red bracelet

Tie ends into a firm square knot. Using needle and thread technique for stringing beads, string a 6mm bead, butterfly bead and another 6mm bead onto each yarn end. Make an overhand knot close to last bead on each. Trim yarn ½"/1.3cm from bottom of last knots. Using the tip of the sewing needle, separate yarn strands to form tassels.

Cloisonné is the fusion
of bronze, glass and
• metal. Chinese
cloisonné, like the
beads featured here,
has been around
since the 1600s.

resources

AS CUTE AS A BUTTON
Suite G
San Diego, CA 92106
www.ascuteasabutton.com
- Buttons and buckles

BEADBOX, INC.
4860 E. Baseline Road
Suite 101
Mesa, AZ 85206
www.beadbox.com
- Beads
- Chain-nose pliers
- Jewelry findings

BERROCO, INC.
P. O. Box 367
14 Elmdale Road
Uxbridge, MA 01569-0367
www.berroco.com
- Yarns

COATS & CLARK
Consumer Services
P. O. Box 12229
Greenville, SC 29612
www.coatsandclark.com
- Cotton thread

CRYSTAL PALACE YARNS
160 23rd Street
Richmond, CA 94804
www.crystalpalaceyarns.com
- Yarns

DMC
77 South Hackensack Avenue
Building 10F
South Kearny, NJ 07032
www.dmc-usa.com
- Cotton thread

DRITZ
Prym Consumer USA Inc.
P. O. Box 5028
Spartanburg, SC 29304
www.dritz.com
- Sewing notions

ECLECTIC ETC., INC.
P. O. Box 10
Willow Grove, PA 19090-0010
www.eebeads.com
- Beads
- Jewelry findings

FIRE MOUNTAIN GEMS AND BEADS
One Fire Mountain Way
Grants Pass, OR 97526-2373
www.firemountaingems.com
- Beads
- Jewelry findings
- Silk thread

JCAROLINE DESIGNS, L.P.
10801 Hammerly Boulevard
Suite 130
Houston, TX 77043
www.jcarolinecreative.com
- Buttons and buckles

JEWELRY SUPPLY INC
301 Derek Place
Roseville, CA 95678
www.jewelrysupply.com
- Beads
- Jewelry findings

LAND OF ODDS
718 Thompson Lane
Suite 123
Nashville, TN 37204
www.landofodds.com
- Beads
- Jewelry findings

SIOUX TRADING POST
415 Sixth Street
Rapid City, SD 57701
www.siouxtrading.com
- Buttons and buckles

SUNSHINE CRAFTS, INC
P. O. Box 516
Safety Harbor, FL 34695-0516
www.sunshinecrafts.com
- Beads
- Wood Beads
- Jewelry findings
- Craft supplies
- Pearls

acknowledgments

I would like to express my thanks to Art Joinnides and Trisha Malcolm for giving me this opportunity to share my designs with crocheters who love jewelry, too.

Many thanks to all who played an important part in bringing **Hooked on Jewelry** to fruition: Diane Lamphron for her beautiful design, David Lazarus and Rose Callahan for their gorgeous photography and Michelle Bredeson for her attention to detail and her enthusiasm. I couldn't be happier.

Special thanks to Margery Winter, Norah Gaughan, Brenda York, Deana Gavioli, and Donna Yacino at Berroco, Inc., for their generous supply of fabulous yarns and their treasured friendship and support.

And to my sister Emily J. M. Harste, who made sure I dotted my i's and crossed my t's.